D░░░░░
MIDSIZED
GROWTH

BOOK 1 > **PEOPLE**

PRESS PROOF | This copy is from the first short run of books produced for initial review by the publisher and author.

DRIVING MIDSIZED GROWTH

BOOK 1 > **PEOPLE**

How the Best Midsized Companies
Systematically Recruit, Develop
and Team their Talent

ROBERT SHER

Author of **MIGHTY MIDSIZED COMPANIES**

ACCLAIM FOR *DRIVING MIDSIZED GROWTH: PEOPLE*

. . . .

"Just as you would never treat a teenager like you would a baby, or even an adult, you can't handle a midsize company like a small start-up or a large corporation. It requires a unique touch. Robert Sher's terrific new book, Driving Midsize Growth, brilliantly distinguishes the critical differences that come with midsize companies and provides 3 critical ways to effectively drive growth. Not surprisingly, his focus is on people, people, people! An excellent read!"

Stephen M. R. Covey, *The New York Times* and #1 *Wall Street Journal* bestselling author of *The Speed of Trust*

"I've spent the past 10 years conducting research on middle market companies, and Rob Sher truly understands the challenges and issues facing these businesses. Through his own experiences running a midsized company, to collecting qualitative examples through conversations with middle market leaders, Rob's ability to translate the critical issues into actionable recommendations is of value to any company. He speaks the language of the middle market".

Doug Farren
Managing Director, National Center for the Middle Market at The Ohio State University Fisher College of Business

"Many midsized leaders I encounter lament that "we're too big to be little, and we're too little to be big." Rob's engaging book reassures, motivates and offers easy-to-implement strategies for those seeking to manage and accelerate their midsized company growth. His relatable examples highlight midsized businesses' unique competitive advantages along with their capabilities and cultures that enable them to control their own destiny."

Steve Gido
Principal, ROG Partners

"Middle market enterprises depend on people to grow, but their busy leaders tend to underinvest in the strategic thinking and execution that will help them find the right people, help them grow, and build the capability to lead. What's brilliant about this book is that Sher understands how to do these things without overburdening a company with process, policy, or procedure. Every executive at a midsized company can benefit from the ideas and insights in this book.

Thomas A. Stewart
Chief Knowledge Officer,
AchieveNEXT and author of
Intellectual Capital

OTHER BOOKS BY ROBERT SHER

The Feel of the Deal; How I Built a Company through Acquisitions

Mighty Midsized Companies; How Leaders Overcome 7 Silent Growth Killers

Copyright © 2021 by Robert Sher

Published by 1 to Ponder

www.1toponder.com

No part of this publication may be reproduced, stored in a system, or transmitted in any form or by any means except permitted under Section 107 or 108 of the 1976 United States Copyright Act, without either the written prior permission of the publisher or authorization through payment of the appropriate fee to the Copyright Clearance Center Inc. in Danvers, MA USA. Phone 978-750-8400 Web: www.copyright com

Disclaimer of Warranty: While the publisher and author have made every effort to be accurate and complete, no such warranty is made, and they specifically disclaim any implied warranty of merchantability and fitness for a particular purpose. Some of the numbers have been changed to protect confidentiality, and some of the names have been changed as well.

Library of Congress Cataloging-in-Publication Data

Sher, Robert 1961-

Driving Midsized Growth: People / by Robert Sher

ISBN-13: 13:978-1-60222-000-3
ISBN-10: 1-60222-014-X
Library of Congress Control Number: 2021941059

DEDICATION

··

*To the leaders of midsized companies everywhere,
who despite all the challenges, get up every day and
strive to build mighty midsized companies.*

TABLE OF CONTENTS

ACKNOWLEDGMENTS

· ·

I am grateful to many who helped through years of research, then book production, teaching, observing, sharing, and helping.

My thanks to hundreds of company leaders who shared their stories, both sad and glad, with openness that allowed me to probe the depths of the growth drivers. Be sure to review the list of business leaders in the Appendix who gave their time in interviews over the past several years.

I must especially thank all my clients, whose challenges and wisdom have taught me much and contributed hugely to this book. A special thanks to Bob Buday of Buday Thought Leadership Partners, my guide to stepping up my game as a thought leader, who contributed in many powerful ways to the creation of the book.

During the research phase I had much support. Our marketing leader, Preety Adams, has been my right hand for research and thought leadership, scheduled countless interviews, extracted critical data from all those interviews, and acts as our internal editor and coordinator of our thought leadership team. She also managed the enormous flow of work as all the interviews were summarized, reviewed, studied, and excerpts approved. It takes a lot to pull the key lessons out of thousands of pages of interview transcripts.

Writer Michelle Rafter did the lion's share of the editing work, taking my ideas, prescriptions, and articles created over the past years during the research phase and turning them into compelling prose. David Rosenbaum, who edited my *Mighty Midsized Companies* book, once again put his final touch on the prose. It never ceases to amaze me that even when I do my best writing, writers and editors like Michelle and David can still make it better.

Many thanks as well to Joni McPherson, our cover designer, and Corefact, our printer, whose technology allowed for and inspired our QR code system.

INTRODUCTION

....

Midsized companies are not simply bigger small businesses, nor are they smaller big businesses. They are their own thing, *sui generis,* and their challenges—and their advantages—are unique to them, not shared by smaller or larger businesses.

Right now, a major challenge confronting all midsized businesses is talent. They are starved for it; they need it to grow, and many simply don't know how to get or develop it.

By the time a company reaches midsized, the people practices it used as a small business are neither adequate nor appropriate, certainly not as a platform for growth. The owner or CEO may realize they have to recruit and retain the best talent to compete with larger or smaller businesses, but he or she often has no idea how to make that happen. And leaving positions unfilled is a guaranteed growth killer.

Even when midsized companies have exceptional people, their leaders usually are too busy to help them develop. That's one of the curses of midsized businesses, especially those on a growth trajectory. Also, as the needs of the business increase, its people may not have the skills to keep up with the new demands created by that growth. They usually don't.

Midsized companies' people problems don't end there. If their best people aren't learning and growing, and aren't enjoying a rewarding work experience, they could leave for greener pastures.

I know all of this because I've experienced these problems as a midsized business owner and I've seen them emerge at the midsized companies I work with in our consulting practice.

And I know there's a better way.

By adopting a few key people practices, midsized companies can attract the talent they need in sufficient quantities to grow their businesses. They can keep them happy. They can even lure people away from much larger companies or appealing startups precisely because they're midsized. That's one of the blessings of being midsized. Call it the Goldilocks factor—for many people, they're not too big, not too small; they're just right.

I've identified three practices that, if done well, will drive a midsized company's growth. These practices—

the people drivers for which I've named this book—aren't borrowed from larger enterprises, which have more money and bigger human resources staffs. Instead, they are the sometimes-overlooked practices that the best-managed midsized companies use to recruit and retain top talent, to develop future leaders, and to create high-performing leadership teams that enjoy working together to grow the business.

This book focuses on leaders. But it also covers the people leaders employ. If you adopt these practices to make your own talent strategies even 10% better than the competition's, that difference in your ability to drive growth will be visible and palpable.

And that will be fun.

Midsized businesses are an economic force

The midsized company market is huge, but information on talent management practices for the midmarket is scarce.

The United States is home to approximately 200,000 midsized companies. Companies that fall into this category have annual revenue of $10 million to $1 billon. Midsized companies are a foundation of the U.S. economy, accounting for a third of private sector GDP and employment. That's according to the National Center for the Middle Market, run by Ohio State University's Fisher College of Business, one of the country's preeminent researchers of the middle-market economy.

Midsized firms have been a powerful engine of economic growth since the Great Recession of 2007-2008. Until the Covid-19 pandemic, they performed better than companies of other sizes by several measures. For example, from 2012 to 2019, midsized companies averaged 6.5% revenue growth compared to 3.5% for large businesses. During the same period, midsized companies averaged 4.3% employment growth, compared to 2.3% at big companies. According to NCMM, midsized company employment growth also outperformed that of small companies.

Of course, the pandemic hurt all companies of all sizes. No one was immune. As I write this in spring 2021, many still aren't out of the woods. But midsized companies contained their losses during the crisis better than both larger and smaller companies. Resiliency is baked into the nature of midsized companies.

Mighty, but invisible

Despite their outsized impact on the national economy, the total number of companies that can be defined as midsized is small. They barely make up 3% of all U.S. businesses. Because there are so few of them, in many ways midsized companies have been invisible, rarely studied or written about.

Why? Along with the fact that they are small in number, midsized businesses often are privately owned by founders who bootstrap their way to becoming bigger businesses rather than taking outside financing. That's why you don't read about them as often in coverage of entrepreneurs and the venture-capital industry. And they're too small to be lumped in with Fortune 500 companies in business-school case studies. There aren't many consultants like me who specialize in midsized companies. The management consulting industry's titans—firms like McKinsey, Boston Consulting Group, and Bain—largely ignore them, partly because midsized businesses don't have millions of dollars to spend on them.

However, their in-between size isn't the only thing (or even the most important thing) that makes midsized companies different. Through my work, I've come up with a half dozen other characteristics that set them apart:

- They have a lower tolerance for risk.

- Their internal communications tend not to be so hot.

- People management practices are rudimentary.

- Leaders have less time to develop.

- Leaders have less time to think strategically.

- Leaders rose as technical experts or entrepreneurs, but without much executive experience.

This may sound negative—and in our research, we've seen some midsized companies get hammered by these problems—but we've also seen others grow like Topsy, avoiding what we have found to be the most dangerous growth killers. We call these companies "mighty," and I wrote about them in my last book, *Mighty Midsized Companies; How Leaders Overcome 7 Silent Growth Killers.*

Most midsized companies need to grow to stay healthy. The status quo is never a friend to the midsized business, as it may sometimes be to the neighborhood mom-and-pop or to the global Fortune 500 behemoth. After all, many small businesses just strive to stay alive to pay a salary to the owner and a few helpers. Massive global companies have access to public markets and the momentum to carry them onward for years. But many midsized company owners and CEOs aspire to grow their businesses to the next level. In *Mighty Midsized Companies*, I examined the seven silent factors that can kill growth and explained how to avoid them. I call them "silent" because they can slip in and set up shop before you realize what's happening. It takes skill to recognize them:

- A lackadaisical approach to time and deadlines

- Needless tinkering with top-level strategies

- Reckless attempts at growth

- Fumbling strategic acquisitions

- Operational meltdowns

- Running out of money

- Tolerating bad leaders

The Nine Growth Drivers for Midsized Companies

The flip side of growth killers is growth drivers. Through my consulting work and the midsized companies that I've researched since *Mighty Midsized Companies*, I've identified nine key areas that midsized companies must focus on to grow. The people drivers this book is about are part of this all-important group.

Before I share more, let me be clear about how I define growth. It means:

- Growth of revenues

- Growth of profits

- Growth of a company's value if it were to be sold

Growth may not happen quickly, but its pace shouldn't be glacial. The big question for most midsized company leaders is what they should do differently to achieve their growth goals, whatever they may be. Our answer is to focus on one or more of the nine drivers.

The Nine Growth Drivers of Midsized Companies

Focus Area: PEOPLE

① Recruiting

Systematically recruit high-quality talent at all levels. Great people—the most talented people—drive growth faster, creating midsized companies that are stronger than their competition. Midsized companies that commit to a systematic recruiting process make talent a competitive advantage.

② Developing Talent

Investing in your highest-potential people drives growth. Our research shows that concentrating professional development initiatives on your highest-potential employees has the biggest impact on your growth. Developing even four or five of your best people moves the needle.

③ Leading with Teams

Teams—not individuals—lead the organization. Growing midsized companies can't scale on the backs of a few heroes. The real heroes are strong teams. The strongest midsized companies intentionally strengthen their teams' ability to perform to consistently drive growth.

The Nine Growth Drivers of Midsized Companies

Focus Area: PLANNING AND EXECUTION

④ Planning and Managing to Plan

Clarity about your direction and the exact steps to get there. A strong plan and implementing that plan are equally important for sustainable, predictable growth. The most successful midsized businesses create strategic plans that look forward 3-5 years, and separate shorter-term operational plans that clarify activities.

⑤ Data-driven Decisions

Successful midsized business can't rely on instinct to grow. Midsized companies are way too complex to make decisions without data. To grow and scale your business, you need systems. Strong systems require collecting accurate data, analyzing it and using it to make decisions.

⑥ Finance Capability

Forward-thinking financial leadership. Hitting ambitious goals requires availability of resources—especially financial resources. Finance and budgeting teams who can accurately forecast what resources will be required to drive growth must play a pivotal role.

The Nine Growth Drivers of Midsized Companies

 Focus Area: GO TO MARKET

⑦ Market Intelligence

Understanding customers, competitors, talent and vendors. The top midsized companies track and analyze shifting marketplace conditions and use that intelligence as a competitive advantage to stay ahead of the competition, anticipate market trends and attract the best talent and partners.

---

⑧ Strategic Growth

New markets, new products and M&A. Significant sustained growth requires strategic growth initiatives. Companies need to look for opportunities to enter new markets, launch new products and attract new customers.

---

⑨ Systematic Sales and Marketing

The right systems and tools deliver predictable, positive results. Achieving sustainable growth requires a selling system with the right people and tools, supported by marketing that puts leads into your pipeline and nurtures them until they are ready to buy.

Midsized company owners and CEOs are aware of these growth drivers but they may undervalue or skip implementing certain aspects of each. That can reduce their effectiveness and negatively affect outcomes. Midsized companies may deploy other means to support growth, including managing operations, leveraging intellectual property or other assets, and so on. But those functions don't necessarily *drive* growth.

Putting systems in place is especially important for emerging midsized companies: companies that are just entering midsized territory, with annual revenue of $15 million to $200 million. As they grow from small to midsized, they need many more people than an owner or CEO can reliably hire through their own networks or local advertising. For talent needs of that scale, companies need systems such as those I'm about to describe.

People drivers

This book homes in on the first three growth drivers: those that pertain to people. Many insights and examples I share are directed to leaders and managers, and in particular to owners and CEOs. Yet much of what you'll read could help anyone at a midsized company, from someone in an entry-level position or their first job out of college to someone years into their career.

Here's an introduction to the three critical people drivers that I will expand upon in the chapters that follow.

Recruiting top talent. Consistently recruiting enough high-quality talent at all levels fuels growth. But many midsized companies struggle with recruiting and settle for people who are nothing more than a good fit. But "a good fit" is not the same as "a great fit." Midsized companies with an abundance of creative, talented people at the top of their class grow markedly faster than their competition. They just do. I've witnessed it. That's why I know it's worth the time and effort to find the great fit.

In Chapter 1, I spell out why it's important to take a systematic approach to finding and signing the best and brightest for your company. This includes using tactics that sales and marketing departments use to prospect for customers. I will discuss short-term tactics to use when your hiring needs are urgent and longer-term strategies that can make your company a consistent magnet for top talent. I illustrate these tactics with real examples, something you'll see sprinkled throughout the book.

Developing talent. Some of your employees are capable and eager to move up as your company grows. They love what they do, love the company, and have bought into your mission. These are your high-potential employees. Actively developing high-potentials reduces the time it takes for them to take on leadership roles. It also increases your pool of potential leaders. Systematically helping high-potential employees earn promotions and increase their responsibilities fuels growth. It's also relatively less expensive and less risky than hiring from the outside.

In Chapter 2, I lay out the professional development that midsized companies with ambitious growth plans must offer high-potential employees, including internal and external training, mentoring and coaching.

Leading with teams. Many small companies succeed and grow on the backs of their owners and founders and other individual heroes. That's great. But that's not how midsized companies grow. A hero can lead, inspire, and solve problems for 10 or maybe even 20 employees. No one can do that for 100. Not well. That requires teams. Excellent teamwork is a hallmark of successful midsized companies where teams at every level work together productively, cohesively and happily.

Chapter 3 explains what it takes to make the transition to team-based leadership. I call this the journey from "I" to "we." I will walk you through the elements necessary to make a team-leadership model work, one that will give top leaders more time to create the long-term plans that drive growth.

Research on midsized company growth backs up what we know from our work: implementing these three people drivers will have a direct and positive impact on growth.

Attracting and retaining talent and staff development are two of seven key management practices and behaviors that drive growth at midsized companies, according to NCMM. Not only that, 71% of midsized companies identified as "growers" (those with year-over-year revenue growth of 30% or more) are adept at attracting top managerial talent. And 64% provide clear career paths for employees.

Feeling overwhelmed? Don't be. Most midsized company CEOs don't have the time nor the resources to institute all three people drivers at all levels, and to every employee. Instead, I encourage them to start by focusing on those high-potential employees. These stars will pull everyone along with them, so focusing on them can have the biggest immediate impact on the business.

Why listen to me?

Before I consulted with midsized companies, I ran one myself. It was my introduction to the power of people as drivers of growth. From 1984 to 2006, I was a founder and the CEO of Bentley Publishing Group. I led the business through four acquisitions that turned it into one of the country's leading decorative art publishers. I wrote my first book, *The Feel of the Deal*, the year after I left Bentley, which merged with another firm to form the Bentley Global Arts Group.

In the 15 years since I formed Mastering Midsized, our firm's business consultants, coaches, and I have helped more than 170 midsized companies tackle many of the same issues that I cover in this book. We worked hand-in-hand with them to turn their people into drivers of growth. Helping those companies provided us with the insights that I'm sharing here. Organizations such as NCMM do commendable work collecting data on midsized companies. And I routinely refer to and depend on their research. But to understand what needs to happen, and what practices need to change, to accelerate midsized company growth, there's no substitute for working one-on-one with midsized company leaders.

I'm a big believer in sharing what I've learned through my involvement in peer organizations and in my writing. I joined the Alliance of Chief Executives, a private group for CEOs, back when I was still running Bentley. I frequently speak at Vistage, a peer mentoring group for CEOs, and groups like it. I've led or participated in hundreds of peer-group sessions. And I've listened to the real-world challenges that midsized company leaders face. And, from their experiences and hard-won wisdom, I believe I've learned how to solve the problems and address the challenges that arise uniquely in the midsize space.

Since 2014, I've written a monthly Forbes.com column on the art and science of running midsized companies, and more than a half dozen articles for *Harvard Business Review*. To write this book,

I conducted research with more than 130 owners, CEOs, and other executives at midsized companies around the country.

How to use this book

This book is designed for executives and managers leading midsized companies. It's especially relevant to CEOs at emerging midsized companies as finding the talent you need to grow is especially urgent. I've also written this book for the owners of privately held or family-owned business, and CEOs of companies with outside funding, as well as for those running a small publicly traded company.

As is the case with some of the companies for which we consult, you could be CEO of a professional services firm—an architecture, accounting, law, or engineering firm—that's owned by one or more partners in the business.

I also have written this book for heads of small businesses knocking on the midsize door, needing to put systems in place to get it to open. And, finally, for midsized companies whose rapid growth has outrun their management capabilities.

I want to help midsized companies of all kinds be more successful in improving their people drivers. *But this is not an HR book.* It's a book about leadership, and how owners and CEOs of midsized companies must hire, develop, and direct people. I firmly believe that if CEOs insert my philosophies about people drivers into their companies' DNA, their business and people will thrive. But if CEOs think of these activities as HR's responsibility, they won't lead the charge to change the ways their businesses hire, develop, and team people to drive healthy growth. And they need to. That said, I believe HR leaders will embrace the philosophies I share and support the actions I recommend.

You'll also see QR codes sprinkled throughout the book. I added them to share more material at no extra cost should you want to delve deeper into specific topics. Just scan the QR code with the camera app on your mobile phone or tablet to see in-depth case studies, videos with CEOs, tools, and more.

So, let's dive into the first people driver: improving recruiting to spot and hire the high-potential employees you will need to push your company to the next level.

AUDIO DOWNLOAD OF THIS CHAPTER

Listen to author Robert Sher read this chapter. Scan this QR code to instantly download and play on your device.

CHAPTER 1

· ·

Recruiting—It's the Talent, Stupid

B ack in 2008, P2S was an ambitious Long Beach, California–based engineering firm with about 75 employees. Today, it has 275 employees, with satellite offices up and down the West Coast. It designs buildings and infrastructure such as a state-of-the-art operating room at the University of Washington's medical center, and it's also automating terminals at the Port of Long Beach, one of the world's most eco-friendly, high-tech container terminals. The company has won industry awards for design and project management.

P2S, in short, is a very different operation than it was a decade ago. Why?

Short answer: People, and the way P2S recruits them.

Back in 2008, when it had job openings, P2S turned to recruiting agencies. And the agencies flooded

P2S's managers with resumes—the better to collect commissions that could reach 33% of a new hire's first-year pay.

But that mountain of resumes didn't always turn into great hires. Of course, it didn't help that P2S's managers weren't very good at describing what they needed, and they really weren't sure what questions to ask candidates in job interviews. It showed. Every year, out of every 20 new employees hired, four or five didn't last 90 days.

P2S CEO Kevin Peterson didn't need to be told that what the company was doing wasn't working. So, bit by bit, he overhauled P2S's hiring approach. He brought on a full-time in-house hiring professional. Managers were trained how to describe jobs and what questions to ask candidates. The company launched a robust summer internship program for engineering majors to identify entry-level prospects. It created buddy and mentorship programs to make new hires feel like they were joining a team.

Peterson also committed to being a "class A employer," offering great benefits, perks, opportunities, and support. That burnished the company's brand and paved the way for a referral program that paid employees up to $10,000 for recommending candidates who stick with the business for at least 90 days.

Today, P2S still taps external recruiters for a few positions, but employee referrals now account for 58% of all new hires. That's a lot. And the internship program brings in another 10%. In fact, its internships are so popular that in 2018, P2S received 1,500 applications for 14 spots in its mechanical engineering internship program. Up to 70% of students who complete the summer program accept full-time positions after graduation, ensuring the company a steady flow of entry-level talent, and creating a buzz about P2S. Since fully rolling out its new approach to hiring, "I can't think of anyone who hasn't worked out," Peterson says.

Why am I going on about P2S and hiring? Why am I starting "People Drivers" here?

Because if there's one thing that our client work has shown, it's that excellence in recruiting is midsized companies' secret to growth and success. The successful midsized companies that we work with see talent as their competitive advantage. Consequently, they work hard on (and pour money and time into) doing the best job of recruiting they can.

Actually, the importance of good recruiting shouldn't come as a surprise. According to the National Center for the Middle Market, companies of $10 million to $1 billion that can boast of top talent outperform their peers significantly and sustainably. We've seen it again and again in the clients we work with, including emerging midsized companies and well-established organizations, in industries of all kinds, everywhere in the country. Companies that can find and hire great people when they need them grow faster and more profitably than those that can't. It's that simple.

Of course, finding the best candidates for critical jobs is neither simple nor easy. Midsized company leaders say that attracting, training, and retaining talent is among their top five challenges. That's especially the case when it comes to staffing upper-level positions.

Peterson, who participates in lots of roundtable discussions with other midsized company CEOs, says it's a constant refrain among his peers: "Every year, it's 'How do you hire? How do you find good people to hire?'"

What this chapter will cover

General best practices for recruiting are well known and shared in enough books, blogs, and podcasts that there's no need to rehash them here.

IN DEPTH ▶ THE P2S INTERVIEW

P2S's successful recruiting program includes internal recruiting, spirit teams, internship and new hire programs, and an interviewing scorecard. Read the full detailed summary of the interview between the author and CEO Kevin Peterson and the analysis and advice on *Forbes*.

Instead, I'm going to zero in on those practices that work best for midsized companies, the strategies that help them compete with smaller outfits and, especially, bigger ones. In this chapter, we cover the ideas and approaches midsized companies can use to hire top people. We look at midsized companies that put these techniques into practice with results that will make you envious.

Executives running midsized companies can take a page from Peterson's book: take a systematic approach to pursuing job candidates the same way you would to recruit customers, using both short-term and long-term strategies.

In other words, recruit employees like you would customers. That sounds good. Let's see what it really means.

Prospect for employees like you prospect for customers

Midsized companies that are successful recruiters use sales and marketing techniques to understand the prospective pool of job candidates. They create personas that will be useful when crafting job ads. And they play up the strengths that come from being larger than smaller businesses and smaller than bigger ones.

Adopt a "funnel" approach to recruiting

When you're selling a product or service, what you're really selling is the various ways in which your product or service is better than the competition's at meeting a potential customer's wants or needs. When you're promoting a new position, it's the same thing. You're selling the reason why your company is better than other organizations at meeting the candidates' wants and needs. To do that, you must think about why people would want to be associated with your company.

Just as sales and marketing identify prospects who are a great fit for a company's products and services, good recruiting finds candidates who are a great fit for your business.

How do sales and marketing do it? They cast a wide net. They assume that marketing campaigns will always have many more misses than hits. Direct mail, email, and other marketing campaigns typically yield response rates of 2% to 5%. Although that rate of return may seem low, it's considered successful enough that the same campaigns are used again and again. Sales also casts a wide net. Only a tiny percentage of the catch become customers, yet we celebrate and continue those methods as well.

Both marketing and sales refer to this as a "funnel"; many leads flow into it but only a few customers come out. Sales and marketing use the funnel in good times and bad, tweaking it as needed to increase the leads that go in to maintain a steady conversion rate. To tailor their efforts to customers' buying habits and increase the number of shoppers they convert to buyers, sales and marketing teams commonly create personas, or categories of customer types.

Now think of hiring. Most midsized companies wait until there's an opening to fill. Then they run an ad and hope to convert a candidate who responds into an employee. If sales and marketing took that approach, the business would go broke pretty quickly. Imagine putting a product on a shelf before looking for someone who might buy it. Overall, 59% of midsized company executives say they wait to recruit until there is a specific position to fill rather than having an ongoing outreach effort to stock talent pools with potential candidates. No wonder midsize company executives are always in a lather when it comes to filling positions.

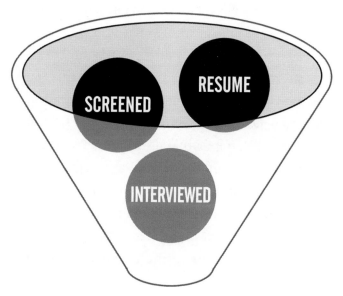

Use personas; envision the ideal candidate

Waiting to act until you need to hire might make sense when a lot of people are looking for work and they're sure to have the skills you need. Today, however, most employees with top skills already have jobs. Of course, those lucky people may not be happy. Maybe they're jovial, fun-loving people stuck in a sterile environment. Or they'd like to be on a small, closely knit team but they're trapped in a huge, global enterprise.

Most midsized businesses have something unique that sets them apart. It could be their size, culture, or passion for a cause. It's up to them to communicate that uniqueness to the people with jobs that aren't ideal for them anymore, so those folks are aware that there are other, better opportunities out there waiting for them. The tool for doing that is the persona.

Personas are profiles of the personalities and attributes of the type of person who would want to work for you, in your sector, at your very unique business. The persona for midsized company management positions is often someone who likes being close to the action, but not necessarily on the front line. They appreciate time frames that allow them to see the start and finish of key initiatives so they see the fruits of their labors, and they want to know the people who will control or co-manage their projects. It's someone who likes to be part of, or lead a team, not a hero who wants to go it alone. It's also someone who may dislike the instability of a startup, or the frustrating bureaucracy of working for a large enterprise.

Using personas is not about creating a list of skills for every mid- or upper-level management job you need to fill; it's more about understanding what connects your brand with the kind of people who would flourish at your company. You'll see how personas can be used in job ads when we talk about them a bit later in the chapter.

The powerful midsized advantage

For some jobs, midsized companies come to the market at a disadvantage. They may not look as hip as some venture-backed startups. They generally lack the brand cachet of a Fortune 500 company. Nor, typically, can they match the compensation and benefits packages larger companies can offer. And many midsized companies are located in smaller towns or less populated areas and have difficulty competing for candidates from large, highly desirable markets.

But when it comes to recruiting, midsized companies have a lot going for them. They have more resources at their disposal than startups or other small businesses, and they can use those resources to create disciplined recruiting processes. They can offer candidates more stability and better compensation than firms smaller than they are. And compared to larger companies, midsized companies feel more intimate. Because they tend to run leaner, there's typically less bureaucracy than there is at larger companies, and more opportunities to rise through the ranks. They also tend to have a stronger connection to the communities in which they're located, a big plus for many younger people.

One of our clients uses its size as a plus in recruiting for management roles. HdL Companies is a revenue, audit, and operations firm in Brea, California, that collects business license fees, hotel taxes, and other revenues for local governments. After 38 years in business, HdL has increased its client base to more than 500 government agencies across the country. Even though it has 200 employees, it's still smaller than the publicly traded companies that it competes with when hiring for positions such as revenue managers. Rather than viewing this as a disadvantage, HdL uses it as a calling card to attract people who've become disaffected in big corporate environments where success is often measured solely by profits. It uses its size to say it is big enough to provide comprehensive service to customers, but nimble enough to adapt quickly to the market and demand.

Employee ownership, core values, flexibility for work-life balance, and a team-oriented culture are other ways HdL uses its size to its advantage. They have fun, laugh, have a good time—all things not typically true for big companies.

HdL staffs its client services department with ex–local government leaders when they retire or choose to move to the private sector. As HdL's client services team delivers its services, it gets to know the client contact personally, maintaining a list of those who would be a good fit for HdL. It gently probes for signs of readiness to exit public service, and when that becomes clear, it raises the opportunity. HdL is always casting its net, keeping the top of the funnel full.

In a recent instance, HdL was recruiting a client services manager who worked for a much larger competitor but had become disillusioned with the bureaucracy that came with her job. That was HdL's cue to play up its integrity-based culture, which is dedicated to innovation, nimbleness, quality customer service, and a collaborative, positive team spirit. It worked. The candidate accepted a position and, according to company officials, has gone on to do great things over the 8 months and running term of employment.

IN DEPTH ▶ VIDEO INTERVIEW OF HDL'S CEO

Learn how HdL's powerful employer brand powers some of their recruiting efforts and hear how they solved a key challenge in an entry level position not helped by their brand. Watch Robert Sher interview CEO Andy Nickerson as well as gain access to other details about HdL's story of transformation and growth.

The short game: quick but powerful tactics

Midsized companies achieve the best recruiting results when they take the long view and make strategic moves that take time and money. But there's also much to be gained from using short-term tactics, especially when you have high-priority positions to fill.

To build a short game, put someone in charge of and dedicated to recruiting, writing effective job ads, and adopting and implementing best practices for the interviewing process. Those include treating job candidates with as much TLC as prospective customers.

Centralize recruiting project management

When there's a need for hiring speed, it helps to have one person in the driver's seat. Setting up an in-house recruiting specialist is not unlike setting up a full-time salesperson to prospect for new customers and sell every day. Unfortunately, a lot of midsized companies don't do that. In part, that's because they tend not to be good at forecasting manpower needs. They aren't big enough to afford to hire people in anticipation of future growth. So, they leave filling positions to managers who just don't do it often enough to become expert. That sets them up to fail. By the time a manager gets the okay to fill a job that's opened up because someone has left or because a bunch of new work has arrived, they're too busy doing their jobs to pursue candidates thoughtfully or aggressively. The result? Companies leave a crucial process to under-trained, overworked managers. Then they wonder why the hiring process is slow and the results meh.

There's a better way. Emerging midsized companies with $15 million to $20 million in annual revenue are big enough to have someone on staff who can focus on hiring full time. Larger midsized companies may be able to afford to have a whole recruiting team.

It's not enough to put just anybody in charge, or to expect an HR generalist to assume recruiting duties on top of their core job. An in-house recruiter hunts for talent; that's a different thing than the typical HR role. They need to do focused, high-quality recruiting as measured against common recruiting performance metrics. Those metrics include cost per hire, time to hire, retention, and how well new hires perform compared with existing talent in the same positions.

An in-house recruiter should also coordinate how job candidates are vetted and be part of final candidate interviews and approvals. The only parts of the process they *shouldn't* lead is specifying role requirements and making the final hiring decision. That should remain a manager's responsibility. Putting an in-house recruiter in charge allows the manager to provide needed input but otherwise be free to do his or her work—which, while there's an opening, is running a short-staffed department. Meanwhile, the in-house recruiter is gaining experience, learning about all the positions in the company.

The experience of one of our clients shows just how valuable an in-house talent expert can be. Kevin Barry Art Advisory (KBAA) creates and supplies artwork to hotels, offices, and other organizations. A few years ago, the company's corporate art galleries in Las Vegas, Los Angeles, and San Francisco faced significant increases in demand. Good problem, right? But client deadlines meant that although the company needed more people, there was little time to devote to hiring. It got so bad that when KBAA got a referral to anyone who could even spell "art," they'd do an interview and make an offer. No surprises, that didn't go so well. KBAA's new hires didn't have the right skills, which put people under a lot of pressure to cover for them. That led to some irritated customers who weren't receiving the service they were used to. The sales team had to pitch in to help. So, sales fell and morale dropped, turning a good thing (increased demand) into a looming catastrophe.

The problems led the company to engage one of Mastering Midsized recruiting managers and put her in charge. It wasn't easy for her. She pushed managers for descriptions of job openings and used one of the company's staff writers to create snazzy job ads. She paid job boards and search engines to list the ads. She monitored incoming applications four times a day and replied to all candidates—good and bad—

the same day. If she needed a manager's input, she pestered them until she got what she needed. She scheduled interviews, follow-ups, and assessments. She kept candidates informed of their progress. She called references. She pushed the process along until an offer letter was sent and accepted.

She was relentless. And it paid off. In six months, KBAA made 26 key hires, increasing the company's total headcount by 52%. Not only did the additional staff help KBAA meet its client deadlines, but the enlarged workforce made it possible for everyone to maintain a better work-life balance.

Once recruiting was up and running, KBAA hired its own recruiting manager who followed our process and continued it, successfully. That's the kind of transformation that can happen when you make one person responsible for recruiting, or, at larger companies, give that responsibility to a dedicated team.

Write snazzy job ads; never post a job description

Don't underestimate the power of a well-written job ad. An ad that explains succinctly why a job is an amazing opportunity, what it entails, and why the company is a great place to work can be the key to attracting candidates that are a great fit. A badly written ad—or worse, a job description posing as an ad—can attract the wrong candidate or fail to attract any qualified candidates at all.

Snazzy job ads go beyond typical job listings by including a wow factor that gets ideal candidates excited enough to contact the company. The persona we talked about earlier in the chapter must be artfully translated into the ad so that when that fabulous candidate reads it he or she feels that it was created expressly for them and they're compelled to check out the opportunity.

These ads should evoke an emotional reaction. They should make the reader want to learn more. They speak to a candidate's motivation for wanting a specific position in a specific kind of company. They are honest and clear about what the company does and what the job entails. They are written in plain language. When writing a snazzy job ad, the key question to ask is, "When my ideal candidate reads it, how will she feel?"

John is a hiring manager at HdL Companies, the California company we just discussed. When John contacted us in late summer 2020, HdL had just six weeks to hire and train 21 customer service representatives before the start of their busy season, when companies can begin to renew annual business licenses. None of the usual places where John posted job ads were working. The firm was down to a trickle of responses, and most were from applicants who didn't have the right qualifications.

We tackled the problem by interviewing three of HdL's best customer service reps. Based on what we learned, we identified four personas with backgrounds that would make them ideal candidates. The personas were: ex–retail workers looking for an office job; inbound call-center specialists; people looking for an entry-level position; and individuals with excellent web search or collections skills. We also identified the keywords to include in the ads so they would pop up in job board search results. We made sure the ads were written in a way that appealed to people who were civic minded, an attribute that might make them want to join a company that worked with local governments.

When we checked with John three weeks later, he said the ad aimed at people looking for their first office job "pulled like mad." Two others yielded a good number of candidates, and one didn't work. Even better, he was surprised and pleased with the high caliber of the candidates compared to those who'd responded to the company's previous ads. He filled all 21 positions despite the time crunch and started their training right on time. The new hires performed well during the seasonal rush, with fewer customer complaints than in the past. "Our ability to staff up on time made a dramatic difference," John says.

Snazzy job ads help fill the recruiting funnel.

But they only need to go so far. Job ads don't need to cover every detail. That can be addressed during the interview. If people apply who aren't qualified, you can always choose not to pursue them. That may mean plowing through more resumes, but that's part of the process. The only purpose of the job ad is to bring candidates to you.

Once you've posted your ad, and applications start pouring in, sort them based on how they fit the criteria you've established for the job. Move fast. Applications with most or many of the attributes you've defined can go into a "yes" pile. Those with some attributes go into a "maybe" pile. Discard the rest. Move the "yes" group through the initial steps of the hiring process quickly as someone else may be poised to snap them up. For the very best candidates, follow up directly with a phone call or an in-person interview. An email could be too slow.

Interview with precision and discipline; don't go by the "feel"

Your hires represent the future of your company. That's true whether you're hiring for the call center, upper management, R&D lab, or retail floor. Once you've weeded out the no-go prospects, you need a process to evaluate the remaining candidates to

SEE FOR YOURSELF ▶ HDL'S SNAZZY JOB ADS

Check out the actual job ads HdL ran to fill 21 customer service openings in a must-fill situation. See how personas tie into job ads to create better candidate pull.

identify a few finalists. You'll want to minimize the time you invest per candidate until you zero in on the best one. Similarly, you may choose to take a more simplified, streamlined approach to interviewing for lower-level positions than for higher-level jobs, matching the investment you make to the risk of a substandard hire. Four rounds of interviews would be overkill for all but the very top positions.

Much has already been written about the best approaches to interviewing, so I won't spend too much time on it here. Instead, I'll zero in on some lesser-known, innovative and powerful tactics.

Create an evaluation form. A form should define the criteria, behavioral attributes, experience, and other qualifications for the job. Use the form to answer the question: What specifics are important to us in selecting the right person? Everyone involved in hiring must be on the same page to objectively assess each candidate.

Capture interview data with rigor. Give it to every interviewer. Insist they use it to grade candidates, taking into consideration three sources of information:

- How the person responds to the interview questions

- Their experience as shown on their resume

- The interviewers' gut reaction based on his or her interactions with the candidate

When you create an interview structure for evaluating candidates based on written criteria, it makes it harder for bias to creep into the process. Bias usually contributes to sub-optimal hiring. You don't want that.

Make interviews as thorough as possible. Put a person with experience interviewing job candidates in charge. Ask the manager looking to fill the position to help the interviewer go deep and apply a systematic approach to collecting the information you need. One method we recommend is top-grading, an interview method that's outlined in a book by the same name. Top-grading is a systematic hiring and interviewing method for identifying the best candidates. It puts candidates through scripted interviews to excavate the details of their past experience.

Here's how top-grading works at Fireclay Tile, a San Francisco Bay Area tile manufacturer. At Fireclay Tile, prospects who make it through two rounds of preliminary screening interviews are invited to a two-hour top-grading interview with at least four people. These interviews include a manager and several potential peers. The panel asks questions about the person's job history and experience that are intended to draw out details about their strengths, weaknesses, and decision-making style, among other things.

Fireclay also uses top-grading interviews to establish a rapport with candidates, which can help reel in top, hard-to-land talent.

Interviews are a crucial part of every hire, but there's more to people than what you can find out in an interview. For that, pre-employment assessments are essential, and well worth the money. We've used many types over the years. Behavioral assessments detect what a person would be like to work with, or how they solve problems. These assessments should never be more than 30% of a hiring decision. Other assessments evaluate a candidate's skills in areas such as math and languages, their ability to multitask, or their knowledge of spreadsheets or a specific programming language. Companies often conduct assessments as part of an initial screening before inviting someone to interview.

There is nothing worse than being surprised and disappointed by a poor hire after investing so much time and effort. If a job requires specific skills, say, writing ability, it pays to test up front. The same

DOWNLOAD EXAMPLE INTERVIEW EVAL FORM

Pull down a no-cost interview evaluation form example you can modify to use in your own interviewing processes.

can be said for behavioral attributes if, for example, you're looking for a specific personality and mindset in a salesperson.

Adnan Lawai, founder and CEO of Folio3, uses a two-part skills test of his own creation to screen software developers and program managers. Candidates first take a general aptitude test focusing on problem-solving, which Lawai describes as a shorter and harder version of the math SATs. If they pass, they're invited to take a written test that could involve working on a programming or design problem. The tests are specific to the tasks included in the job. And they work. "What we found over the years is that the test is just a fantastic indicator of how well developers will do on the job," Lawai says.

Even rejected candidates should say good things

Just as a good salesperson advocates for the customer, a recruiter must be an advocate for job candidates. They must cheer them on and keep them informed of their progress and their chances of being hired. Creating an exceptional candidate experience takes effort—especially if you extend that to the candidates you aren't moving forward with. But how you treat the candidates you don't hire will affect your brand. Being respectful increases the chance that candidates who *don't* get an offer leave you feeling good about the experience and the company. They might answer another posting in the future for which they are a better fit. Or they may refer a friend. Treat them badly, you close off those opportunities.

For the candidates you want to move through the funnel, keep them close. Build the connection. That could be the difference between saying yes or no to an offer.

Fireclay Tile takes this approach. The company includes at least four people in candidate interviews, including managers and peers, not only to be comprehensive but also to start building a personal relationship and a sense of community. "Once we've extended an offer, we ask our entire hiring team to reach out and say congratulations," says Eric Edelson, Fireclay's CEO. "We ask them all to say, 'Hey, we love you, we want you to join us'—really pour on the kindness." In many cases, Edelson says, the feedback is, "That was an incredible process. I can't believe how personal it was. I feel like I got to understand the company and really understand the job." Someone who feels like that is well-disposed to getting on board.

Creating an exceptional interview experience can be especially useful when courting passive candidates; employed and talented people who are considering a move. Edelson tells the story of one recent hire who was working at a major competitor. She was happy, but she had heard good things about Fireclay. So, she applied, somewhat casually. She had a fantastic interview during which she talked to a lot of people. She loved the company's brand, and what customers said about it. "We sent her a very thoughtful offer, and we all called her and congratulated her; we overwhelmed her with kindness," Edelson says. "And she accepted!"

Creating a great interview experience sometimes requires making an extra effort to get the candidate to say yes. This could include being available to answer their questions or to set them up to talk to the people they'd be working with if they joined. If relocation is part of the offer, it could mean having someone drive them around the area to get a feel for what it's like. It could also mean bringing in the CEO to close the deal.

Ideal Innovations needed a special intervention by the CEO to wrap up one recent hire. The Arlington, Virginia, government contractor was in advanced talks with a perfect candidate for a vital, hard-to-fill position. However, the candidate was

IN DEPTH ▶ THE FIRECLAY INTERVIEW

Read in detail how they encourage passive candidates to leave good jobs to join Fireclay

and how they use their employer brand powerfully. Read the full detailed summary of the interview between the author and CEO Eric Edelson and the analysis and advice on *Forbes*.

hesitant. He asked questions about provisions in the employee contract, and even had a lawyer review the agreement. No matter how many reassurances the company gave him, he was stuck on the fence about accepting the offer.

That's when the hiring team asked the CEO to intervene. The CEO gained enough of the candidate's confidence for the person to concede that the real sticking point was the cost of relocating. The CEO offered a modest relocation allowance, and the candidate promptly signed on.

"That was a really important hire for us, and no one else could have gotten it," says Ideal Innovations COO Richard Syretz, who has used the same approach selectively with a 100% success rate. "When the CEO weighs in, it establishes a level of trust. What comes across is the CEO's passion for the company. He's the decision-maker. He can address the job, the salary, relocation costs, or whatever the real issue is, and he can get the deal done."

The Long Game: Strategies for Success

Short-term hiring tactics work, but they only get a company so far. Sure, you can write job ads that sparkle and spend $5,000 on a recruiting effort. But it takes a strategic, long-term approach to make the business a talent magnet. With that, you'll always have a list of candidates who will jump at the chance to work with you. You also might not need to spend that $5,000 every time you need to make a hire.

Remember the idea of approaching recruiting the same way that you approach marketing and sales? Success comes when you commit and follow a well-conceived process. Create a strong employer brand, dedicate an adequate budget line to recruiting, track the results, and work those connections with job candidates.

If you plan to grow, taking these steps builds a powerful foundation. It takes time and commitment at the start. And it could be a year or two before you start seeing the dividends. But once the flywheel is spinning, it will begin to deliver results that keep coming with less expense and effort on your part. Not only that, you'll gain a distinct and durable talent advantage over your competition.

Attract the best with your employer brand

Midsized companies know that when sales prospects have a positive perception of the company it makes selling faster and easier. The same thinking applies to prospective employees and a company's employer brand. Employer brand is your company's image and reputation with prospective candidates, current employees, and the general public. Seventy-nine percent of midsized company executives believe that having a good employer brand is essential to their ability to attract top talent.

Small companies may hire so infrequently that it isn't economical to spend on their employer brand. But for emerging midsized companies, that kind of brand-building will definitely contribute to growth. Midsized organizations with strong employer brands capture better talent, and thus report significantly higher average revenue and recruiting success than their counterparts.

How to shape and promote your employer brand is a topic worthy of its own book. For our purposes, let's assume cultivating a strong employer brand includes how the company and its employees create a culture that makes everyone more successful. To activate your employer brand, you must live it, then push it out into the community.

Ascent Environmental uses its employer brand as its primary recruiting tool. The Sacramento, California-headquartered company positions itself as an expert in the environmental service industry by having leadership and other staff speak at conferences, lead trainings, and write articles for industry publications. The goal is to attract like-minded individuals who would want to work alongside acknowledged experts and eventually become thought leaders themselves. Ascent's brand has thought leadership at its core.

From 2010 to 2017, the firm got enough employment inquiries from its employer brand efforts to increase its workforce from five to 70 people with minimal recruiting effort. It's only been in the past few years that the firm added other recruiting best practices to fill a few hard-to-find leadership positions. Even so, it still doesn't use outside recruiters.

Once you envision your employer brand, you must live it. Walk the talk; live your values; honor your promises. Employer brand isn't marketing-speak. New hires, like new customers, can quickly detect empty boasts. They'll leave. They'll talk. And so much for your employer brand.

Once you have established your employer brand, let your marketplace know about it. Use your website, and specifically your careers page. Run video testimonials from current employees. Talk it up at industry conferences, colleges, or other places where you recruit.

Property management company HNN Associates is a good example of a company that lives its employer brand. HNN Associates is a subsidiary of DevCo, a privately held real estate investment company in Bellevue, Washington. Part of DevCo and HNN Associates' stated mission is to build relationships with the community and give back. To that end, HNN regularly participates in local community efforts to provide shelter for homeless families. HNN gives employees 16 hours a year of paid leave time for volunteer work and offers its personnel a 20% housing discount. "I like the fact that they pay you for it so we can all donate our time and help the community out," says Chris, an HNN groundskeeper.

As with building a customer brand, building an employer brand requires taking a long-term view and investing resources with the expectation that results will not come immediately. That's okay. Some things take time. Some things reward that time. A company's employer brand dovetails with its customer brand, as the two are halves of the same whole and they support each other.

A written recruiting budget says you mean business

Many midsized firms claim to have a recruiting budget. But for too many, that just describes an intention to budget, a willingness, "when the time is right," not a commitment to investing. Not surprisingly, those kinds of budget intentions tend to fall by the wayside when different business priorities crop up.

Sales and marketing have real budgets. Recruiting needs one too, with accounts for employer brand-building, communications, internal recruiting staff or administrative recruiting support, and outside recruiters as needed. Without a written budget, you're

IN DEPTH ▶ THE ASCENT ENVIRONMENTAL INTERVIEW

Read how they dominate their sector by recruiting and collecting thought leaders. Read the analysis and advice on *Forbes*.

not serious. With one, you're committed to growing your top and bottom line. You're also committing to growing your team with the best people you can find. That won't happen with last-minute, ad-hoc spending when (or if) cash is available.

A recruiting budget should be a written commitment with detailed monthly goals and spending. To create a recruiting budget:

Create your ideal org chart a year out. Determine who will fill each position, including any planned promotions. That will reveal the extent and timing of your future hiring needs.

Segment positions by cost to fill. Entry-level positions and jobs with large available talent pools are less expensive to fill than positions requiring hard-to-find combinations of skills and experience. Those require additional budget. Expenses dedicated to filling these positions could include covering travel expenses for interviews, referral fees, multiple postings, relocation costs, or signing bonuses.

Determine when outside help is warranted. Filling certain high-level, critical jobs may require hiring an outside recruiter that specializes in specific job functions or upper-management roles. If your ongoing hiring needs are great enough, your recruiting budget could include the cost of hiring a full-time in-house recruiter or other staff, plus onboarding and training of new hires.

Most midsized firms turn to executive recruiters for C-suite or other high-level positions. Their fee is often 33% of the first-year salary. That's expensive, but worth it for a top candidate. On the other hand, if a company always has a number of hard-to-fill positions open, it may be more cost effective to pay an internal recruiter than continue to pay a commission to outside agencies.

Bringing recruitment in-house and developing candidates organically can attract better quality personnel who stay longer and contribute to enhanced corporate performance. In the past, P2S, the Long Beach, California, engineering and commissioning company, had four external recruiting firms on speed dial to fill six to 10 job openings at any given time. To cut back on complexity and gain more control over the hiring process, the company brought most of its recruiting efforts in-house. That includes an employee referral program that pays up to $10,000 for staff who recommend candidates who come to work for the business. Since instituting the changes, 58% of the firm's new hires (as previously noted) come from employee referrals, 34% through the company's website, social media, or internet advertising, and only 8% from outside recruiting. Although the employee referral program payouts are significant, the process costs less in aggregate and has yielded better candidates.

Measure both activity and results

Sales and marketing measure their funnel and conversion rates. That tells them how well they're doing. They also have tools to track prospects. Recruiting should do the same. Many human resources information systems or HR management suites have recruiting applications, including systems for tracking job applications. Scores of stand-alone applicant-tracking systems (ATS) are also available for businesses of all sizes, including midsized companies.

Regardless of what process or tool you use, you'll gain the most insights into your recruiting efforts by tracking:

- Average days from the decision to hire until the person's first day, also known as time-to-fill. This will measure the overall success of the recruiting function as every day that a position is unfilled is hurting your company's potential growth and success.

PEEK AT A TYPICAL RECRUITING BUDGET

 Download this mini-guide to help you create a quick recruiting budget. We've outlined common categories of spending for a recruiting budget. No cost.

- Average qualified resumes you get for each advertised open position. This measures the effectiveness of your outreach.

- Average number of strong candidates you bring into a final round of interviews. Having a choice of great candidates produces far superior results than hiring the only person who wasn't rejected.

- Percentage of new hires who remain on the job for more than six months. Recruiting isn't just about speed; it's about quality. A bad hire is worse than a postponed hire.

- Open positions at any one time. The more open positions you have translates into growth deceleration. This metric is your call to action.

- Percentage of job offers rejected. Even an amazing recruiting function may not work if your company isn't winning the battle against other employers. A high percentage of rejections is a signal to up the ante. Perhaps you need to raise wages and increase benefits. Maybe your employer reputation needs polishing. Something you're doing is not working.

Don't waste the relationship with good talent; stay connected with all finalists

There are people out there who don't work for you now who could be amazing employees in the future.

You know who they are because you met them in the process of hiring someone else. Too many midsized companies abandon these connections when they've filled the position. What a waste!

Remember the strong candidates who made it to the final round but for whatever reason didn't get the job. Don't forget the people who would have been a great fit but weren't quite ready to make a change. Don't discard their applications or let the relationship you've established wither away. Things change. The time may not be right now, but someday...

Keep in touch with them instead of hoping they'll notice the next time you post a job ad. Then you'll be able to reach out to them when you have a suitable opportunity. Creating an ongoing relationship also increases the chances that when they're ready for a new position, your company will be the first one they contact.

In a nutshell, maintaining connections makes you a talent magnet. This means creating a perpetual recruiting machine.

How do you make that happen? By creating a database of potential candidates. Add to it as you get inquiries or come across potential candidates while filling a job opening. An ATS system or CRM application can help recruiters track prospects in this way. Some companies use LinkedIn for this purpose.

It's crucial to have an in-house recruiter to do this work. When they aren't filling positions, they can pivot to the work of building relationships with prospects. That way, when both parties are ready, hires can happen very quickly. And that's what you want.

Continued outreach to prospects keeps your employer brand fresh in their minds. It might take a year, or two, or even 10 for the stars to align until that great candidate is ready to join your company. It can be worth the wait.

In addition to maintaining a database, stay top of mind by adding these prospects to mailing lists, connecting with them on LinkedIn and other social media, inviting them to events, sponsoring industry associations, and more.

Is this any different than a persistent salesperson staying in touch with a prospective but hesitant customer? No. Winning midsized companies stay

IN DEPTH ▶ THE FUTURE STATE INTERVIEW

They put "party" into the recruiting process and have perfected the art of keeping candidates connected. Read the full detailed summary of the interview between the author and COO Kathy Krumpe and the analysis and advice on *Forbes*.

close to both future customers and employees in the same way. They are always ready to close.

Tactics for staying connected don't need to be complicated. Future State, a 75-person consultancy group in Oakland, California, maintains a list of its hottest prospects that the company refers to as the "jalapeño list." The firm contacts prospects on the list whenever it hires for specific projects. Between job openings, Future State organizes events and does follow-up communications to stay in touch and "for us to get to know them better and vice versa," says Kathy Krumpe, the firm's chief operating officer.

Keeping in touch with prospects has led to great results for Nick Montgomery, human resources director at EWI, an applied R&D engineering services company in Columbus, Ohio. Montgomery once identified a prospect who worked at a national lab and had an outstanding reputation in the industry. When Montgomery reached out, the person was interested but in the middle of an important assignment. She wasn't ready. Montgomery stayed in touch. A few months later, the candidate's assignment was over and she was looking for a new opportunity that involved more client engagement. Which was exactly what the EWI position called for. It wasn't long before Montgomery was welcoming the candidate to EWI. "Recruiting is very much like buying a house," Montgomery says. "Sometimes the house you want isn't on the market, so you have to wait. Timing is everything, in life and recruiting."

Don't tinker with your long-term strategy

Once you've laid the foundation for a long-term recruiting strategy, resist the urge to tinker with it too much. Brand building requires continuity and commitment. You can't make sharp turns or flip initiatives on or off. Don't get excited about a brand-building tactic if you're not willing to stick with it. Either commit to executing your long-term strategies with discipline over the long term, or don't waste your time.

Why do some midsized companies tinker with their recruiting strategy? They do it when faced with cash shortages or when they get distracted by other challenges. Then they revert to the reactive behaviors common to small businesses. When a small business needs people, it scrambles to recruit. When it doesn't need people, it shifts resources elsewhere. Small businesses can win by being good scramblers, but midsized companies cannot.

At midsized companies, it's never been more important to have top performers on your teams. If

IN DEPTH ▶ THE EWI INTERVIEW

Discover what a great recruiter does to work the long game and maintain great connections with top talent until they come aboard. Read the full article detailing EWI's recruiting technique and advice on *Forbes*.

you want to grow, you must commit to recruiting the best people quickly and effectively. You can't do that if you're not thinking ahead.

Never Stop Recruiting

No growth-oriented company ever turns off sales and marketing. The same should hold true for recruiting. Even if you're not actively looking for candidates for open positions, keep recruiting because great people are available at different times, not necessarily when you post a job ad.

You want great candidates to know your company and that you're interested in them. When you do that, you'll be the first one they call when they're ready.

Sometimes hiring *ahead* of demand is the wise thing. Hiring a talented person six months earlier than you need him is less expensive in the long run than hiring a *less* qualified person on your schedule, then suffering the consequences. In slow growth times, you can put recruiting on simmer if you must, and then bring activity back to a boil when you have open positions. When on simmer, use the extra time to fertilize the connections you've been cultivating. Use your ATS, LinkedIn, or even a customer relationship management tool to build and maintain a list of "hot" candidates, so when the next hiring surge happens, you're ready to pull from the pool you've stocked.

A solid employer brand can support always-on recruiting. HdL Companies' solid employer brand has so many people approaching the company about jobs that CEO Andy Nickerson has his pick of the best. He gets calls on a regular basis from top talent in his industry looking to join up. That's what I call an advantage.

Fireclay, the California tile maker, built an always-on recruiting strategy around its designation as one of few design companies to have earned a B corporation certification as a socially and environmentally responsible business.

"Having a framework of social responsibility and being very clear about it is something that many, many people have been very excited by," Fireclay CEO Eric Edelson says. "We are able to hire people away from larger companies because they want to work for a brand that is producing something beautiful and also achieve something special for the world, together, rather than just making and selling tile and focusing on profit."

Remember: To build a robust flow of great candidates, treat recruiting as you do sales and marketing. Understand the prospective pool of job candidates. Use personas to craft job ads. Play up the strengths that come from being like Goldilocks: neither too small nor too large but just right, midsized.

Bring both your recruiting short game and long game. Your short game should focus on the low-hanging fruit, the elements of your hiring strategy that can be easily fixed and implemented. That includes centralizing recruiting management, writing better job descriptions, and improving your job interview techniques. You can make big strides in all those areas in just one to six months. They'll all move the needle toward getting more good candidates sooner.

Improving your long game isn't as easy. But it can have a big impact, year after year, and in some ways it can be less expensive in the long run. Upping your long game involves building or refining your employer brand, cultivating relationships with candidates, and budgeting for ongoing recruiting efforts.

Companies will have different starting points for implementing these recommendations depending on where they are in filling all the seats in their organizational chart for the coming year. If you're not sure where to start, and you have many open positions now, pick one element of your recruiting short game. Start with the weakest link in your candidate recruiting funnel and take it from there. If you're in good shape now but you anticipate high growth over the next few years, go strategic and start playing the long game.

MORE RECRUITING READING

We've studied the subject of recruiting functions in emerging midsized companies for some time. If you want to dive in more, scan the QR code for more articles and research, assessments, and other assistance.

MORE COPIES OF THIS BOOK?

Does someone you know need to read this chapter? Of course, you can order a book for them online, but if they're out of stock, or you need quantities, want to drop ship to many different locations, or this is related to a peer group or speaking event, scan this code.

WANT *TO TALK* ABOUT RECRUITING?

Mastering Midsized provides support and guidance for midsized companies who need to improve their recruiting processes. Scan this QR code for the fastest route to talk to someone about getting help.

AUDIO DOWNLOAD
OF THIS CHAPTER

Listen to author Robert Sher
read this chapter. Scan this QR
code to instantly download
and play on your device.

CHAPTER 2

. . . .

A Commonsense Guide to Professional Development

The future success of your company depends on keeping your employees' skills up to date. That's an essential people driver. But the truth is, emerging midsized companies—those with revenues between $15 million and $200 million—aren't all that good at professional development. In fact, after 15 years of working with these companies across the country, I'd say most of them are pretty bad at it. That needs to change.

Owners and CEOs typically don't begin to get their arms around skills development until their revenue is close to $200 million. That's when they start to build out their human resources departments and bring on learning and development specialists. Leaders of companies smaller than that generally feel they're too busy to make professional development a priority.

The research bears this out. On average, only 36% of all midsized companies, with revenue between $10 million and $1 billion, make an effort to help employees upgrade their skills or knowledge. That includes managerial, technical, or everyday business skills such as salesmanship, spreadsheeting, writing, customer service, and similar business functions. I'd wager most of that 36% is happening at companies at the larger end of the spectrum. Even fewer midsized companies—less than a quarter—prepare employees for another job within the organization.

The result is employees who are stuck. Their skills get stale, and pretty soon they don't have what it takes to continue working in their growing, increasingly complex organization. That hampers their company's ability to grow.

When owners or CEOs realize that employees with outdated skillsets and knowledge are holding the organization back, becoming inefficient and making poor decisions, they may have to choose between paying for crash courses to upskill people or spending on outsiders who have the skills they need, with the risk that the new hire—no matter how much screening you do—might not be a good fit. Hiring outsiders also risks alienating employees who may (justifiably) feel they could have done the job if they had just been given the proper tools and a chance.

This is a big problem. And our advice is: Don't try to fix the whole thing.

Instead, concentrate professional development on the core of your workforce, the people who have the biggest impact on your business, your high-potential employees. These are the people who are capable of moving up, capable of taking on more responsibility. Once you get good at elevating your high-potential employees, then you can consider broadening your development efforts.

Helping high-potentials from day one

For one emerging midsized company, it made sense to recruit high-potential graduates right out of college and begin developing them immediately.

Twenty years ago, JLG Architects was a small commercial architectural firm in North Dakota whose four equity partners in the closely held firm wanted to grow. And they intuited that they could use professional development and high-potential employees to do so.

To start, the partners ramped up their recruiting at North Dakota State University's architecture school, targeting graduates for entry-level jobs. Instead of bringing on the occasional new graduate, they hired five or six a year, recruiting from the top 10% of the graduating class. Then they put them through a fast-track training program. Recruits learned about building technology and construction, and the tools and processes JLG used. Newcomers also were coached on soft skills, such as how to collaborate and get along with coworkers, and they participated in a training curriculum built to help them meet professional licensing requirements as fast as possible.

As part of its professional development program and coinciding with JLG's transition to open-book management practices, the firm launched a peer resource group for all employees. Group members met at least once a month to hear experts from across the company talk about ongoing projects and firm operations.

The training program and peer resource group helped the firm's newer architects shave more than a year off the national average for getting licensed. In the first four years that JLG focused on high-potential entry-level hires, the firm more than doubled its head count from 40 to 85. Over that same period, revenue grew five-fold, from $3.1 million to $15 million.

The firm has continued to grow. Since 2011, JLG has expanded from five offices to a dozen offices across four states and has been named one of the country's "Architecture Giants" by Building Design + Construction for the past six years, with over 150 full- and part-time employees.

This story is a testament to the transformative power of professional development, and what can happen when a company pours resources into advancing the skills and careers of high-potential employees.

What this chapter will cover

JLG's success reveals the two pillars of professional development that midsized companies with ambitious growth plans must offer high-potential employees. The first is creating career paths, a process through which high-potential employees can get ahead. The second is mentorship and training.

Preparing today's high-potentials to be tomorrow's managers and technical leaders is especially important for midsized companies that want to grow. Assessing the success of your efforts on an ongoing basis is equally critical. JLG runs its program on a grander scale than most midsized firms, but don't be intimidated. The same general principles apply regardless of your organization's size.

IN DEPTH ▶ THE JLG ARCHITECTS INTERVIEW

JLG Architects enjoys a steady stream of strong talent thanks to their internal development program. Read the full detailed summary of the interview between the author and CEO Michelle Mongeon Allen and the analysis and advice on *Forbes*.

Philosophy: Train your high-potential employees first

Small companies rarely do any kind of training or professional development, and there's often little room to promote people. Many big companies, on the other hand, try to develop everyone, but professional development at those organizations can feel commoditized and rote. Big company managers may not stay in their roles long enough to make their direct reports feel connected to the training or convince them that it is an organizational priority. The path to the C-suite is long. All of it can leave high-potential employees feeling alienated.

If midsized companies make the effort, they can deliver professional development better than either big or small companies. They can provide high-potential employees with customized programs and reward them with one-on-one coaching and challenging work assignments. They can provide their high-potentials with more realistic career paths as they can see that the distance to important, coveted roles is relatively short.

Helping high-potential employees advance their careers is a win-win for midsized companies. If you can help four or five of your best people to become company rock stars, you significantly increase the chances that your company's growth will rocket up the charts.

How do we define and identify high-potential employees?

Since there's so much riding on these people, and I'm recommending that you concentrate your development efforts on them, it's important to know who they are.

How to spot high-potential employees

When you're evaluating both employees and candidates, be on the lookout for indicators that a candidate may be a high-potential employee. On resumes, you can spot them from their history of promotions, or the progress they've already made in their career in your company. If they're at the entry-level, you may see it from their performance in college and related work or internships, from behavioral pre-employment assessments, and from how well they do in the job interview.

In interviews, you can detect high-potential prospects by how they answer questions about their career plans. They might tell you how they someday want to run the company. That's a classic high-potential employee answer. In meetings you'll see them raise their hand often, volunteering for new assignments.

Use assessments to detect behaviors and thinking styles that indicate someone's ability to work at a higher level. When my team and I worked with KBAA, the corporate art consultancy, we used an assessment to measure the behaviors and thinking of the company's four top art consultants. From the results, we created profiles for the company to use as a hiring guide. When the company assessed job candidates as part of the interview process, we tracked how closely they came to the profile. Most candidates were at least 15 years younger than the company's top performers, and many were fresh out of design school, but by comparing them to the profile we could see what they had under the hood and pinpoint the candidates most likely to succeed.

I've already suggested that these are people capable of taking on more responsibility within the organization, including management roles. (They also may be people who want to become experts in their chosen fields without taking on management responsibilities. They could turn into chief researchers, software developers, or lead architects. You get the idea.)

Personally, I have a bias for employees who have the potential to become leaders. Leaders help figure out the path to growth and pave the way for everyone else. Developing leaders is especially important for emerging midsized companies, those organizations with $15 million to $200 million in revenue. Companies in the formative years of building out their management and operations need bench players who can work their way into the starting lineup. There's no better way to do that than by investing in high-potential employees.

High-potential employees aren't the same as high-performing employees. The term "high performing" often is used to describe people who are excellent in their current position but lack either the capability or drive (or interest) to do much more. Think of a sales rep or software developer who loves his job and wants nothing more than to stay put. If they feel that way, it's not critical for them to learn about (or train for) the next position they could hold.

> **High-potential employees aren't the same as high-performing employees.**

Nor are high-potential employees synonymous with high-impact jobs. Companies of all sizes have high-impact jobs, positions that create extraordinary value. Big companies can sometimes lose track of them and, as a result, fail to staff them appropriately. Most emerging midsized companies know exactly which jobs are high impact. But they may think their work is done when they've slotted a high-potential or high-performing employee into the job. Yes, midsized companies need a strong performer in each high-impact role. But they also need a high-potential employee—who may not now be in a high-impact role—as a successor, learning

> **High-performers are people who are excellent in their current position but lack either the capability or drive to do much more**

about that high-impact job, and ready to step in as needed.

Why it pays for midsized companies to focus on their high-potentials

Organizations need both high-performing and high-potential employees. But it's my position that midsized companies are best served by focusing development efforts on the latter.

Why? High-potentials are rarely unemployed. Recruiting them can be expensive. And new hires can be risky because, for many reasons, success is never a given. It is less expensive and less risky to identify a handful of high-potentials in your organization and prepare them to move from one level to the next.

Expediting the development of high-potential employees, especially for high-impact roles such as management or technical leadership, not only helps you grow faster with the talent you have, it helps you keep that talent longer. Training and other forms of professional development for high-potential employees are known to contribute to retention, according to the National Center for the Middle Market (NCMM). Despite that, 61% of midsized companies, and in particular companies on the smaller end of the midsized spectrum, lack policies or processes for career advancement.

Training Regularly Provided

	Managerial	Professional/ Technical
Upgrade skills or knowledge	44%	40%
Teach basic job skills (office) software, work habits, or management practices)	30%	30%
Teach new specific work skills (how to use equipment, machinery, or technical procedures	24%	37%
To prepare for another job (or assignment) within the organization	24%	27%
None of these	14%	14%

Now here's some hard truth. A professional-development program will help your high-potential employees rise through the ranks. When they hit a ceiling in your company, they may very well leave, taking all the skills and training you've provided with them out the door. You hate that. I hate that. But I've found that in the two or three years in which these high-potential employees learn and develop their new skills and capabilities, they are excited, empowered, and working with tremendous focus. That oomph is a powerful growth driver. After that, however long they stick around is a bonus.

That's why it makes sense to provide high-potential employees with professional development even though eventually they may decide they yearn for more challenges than you can provide.

Here's another reality check. You're kidding yourself if you think that you can convince high-potential employees that they're in the best jobs they'll ever get. It doesn't work like that. The era when people spent years in a job, selflessly loyal to their employer, is long gone. If they really are high-potentials, recruiters are calling them, and their friends and families want them to aim high and make the most of their careers. In a world as connected as ours, it's never been easier to see who's hiring and who's paying. The surest way to keep high-potentials (and high-performers) is for your company to be known for providing opportunities for personal and career growth.

How should I begin?

Developing high-potential employees doesn't usually start with grooming them for C-suite positions. It should start where your company's organization chart is weakest. It could be a department leader with no apparent successor. Or someone who's a single point of failure, meaning, if they exit, no one is ready to do their job. In fact, it's any high-impact position without a successor who's prepared and waiting.

Career pathing: Creating a highway for excellence

Many midsized companies treat hiring as the end of a process, rather than what it really is: the beginning. If today's digitally empowered employees don't get the professional development they need, especially the high-potentials, they're apt to map out their career on their own. This often means moving to a new company.

Organizations can address this by creating career paths for their high-potentials. A career path identifies positions to which an employee can reasonably aspire. It also:

- Spells out the skills they need to master to be promoted, in much the same way that you earn course credits in college to advance to the next year.

- Identifies where the person is on the defined path, to determine what their development starting point should be.

- Accounts for those roles where the organization needs talent to grow.

To see how career pathing works, let's look at a hypothetical example of a high-potential employee working as an assistant marketing manager. This person writes well, has solid ideas, and gets along with clients and coworkers. She isn't as good at staying on budget or meeting deadlines. The next job on her career path is marketing manager, a position in which meeting budgets and deadlines is, well, a big deal. As part of advancing to the next level, the assistant may be assigned to manage a major website redesign project where bringing the job in on budget and on schedule will be a big part of calling it a success. That's career pathing.

For career pathing to work, managers must be on board with the process. As this example illustrates, managers can use a high-potential employee's career path to identify work that fills in gaps in their knowledge, skills, or expertise. Managers can also help with training, mentoring, or coaching. They should schedule regular check-ins to make sure a high-potential direct report is progressing and learning as expected, so they can adjust and define next steps. We'll look a little more deeply at assessing how high-potentials are progressing a bit later in the chapter.

HR professionals reading this will say that companies should create career paths for every employee. In a perfect world, that's what we'd do. But at most midsized companies, the resources for professional development are limited. If they try to do everything, they accomplish less, the effort invariably stalls, and no one gets a career path. That's why I advise beginning with a handful of employees you've identified as having high leadership potential.

A career path does not always equal a promotion

Designing career paths is often thought of as the means to a specific end: promotions. But that doesn't have to be the goal. Frankly, midsized companies don't have that many management layers, so the potential for promotions is limited. And not everyone wants to be the CEO. A career path could include giving high-potential employees opportunities for lateral shifts, or a move to a different department.

By definition, your high-potential employees are susceptible to boredom. They want to grow and learn new things. The real building blocks of a career path are skills and competencies. So, to give these people what they want, give them opportunities to learn. While they're at it, they could improve processes, making a company better.

As we saw with JLG Architects, creating a career path for high-potential employees isn't limited to upper-management jobs or skilled professionals.

At Corefact, a Hayward, California, direct-mail marketer, all entry-level employees working in the company's printing facility earn points when they master different production processes. The more points they earn, the more responsibilities they are eligible to assume. And the more responsibilities they can handle, the higher their hourly pay. The company created career paths that climbed right up to lead positions and shift supervisors who support the plant manager. In other words, Corefact has created a talent pipeline that makes it easier for high-potential talent to get recognized with pay, job enrichment, and, in a few cases, promotion.

There's another reason why midsized companies should create career paths for high-potential employees even when a promotion isn't guaranteed. Companies need to groom successors long before people in high-impact roles leave. You never know when someone may get sick, become unable to work, or win the lottery and retire. Even the boss—which could be you—will one day have to figure out when it's time to move on. If you wait for an emergency or an urgent need to arise to develop career paths for stand-out people, your process will be rushed and suboptimal—a case of too little too late. Either your successor won't be ready, or they'll have already quit. And unanticipated gaps between strong leaders in key roles can do significant business damage, especially to midsized companies.

It's important to be aware that you may encounter some high-potential employees who are purely transactional, unwilling to be trained unless there's something in it for them. They might say, "Sure, I'll learn something new… if you guarantee me a raise and promotion." That should be a warning sign. Midsized firms need great team players, not divas.

Keep high-potentials around by keeping them challenged

Remember how I said that high-potential employees can reach a point where they've run out of challenges and leave? It happens, but it doesn't have to. Creating career paths can help hang onto those high-potentials. And doing so can be a runway for a company to expand.

Kevin Barry Art Advisory used career paths to keep high-potential employees challenged, and the company grew as a result. KBAA, the art consulting firm I introduced in the previous chapter, has long hired design-school graduates to work as associate art consultants. The company uses assessments to find and hire people with critical thinking skills and behavioral traits similar to their top employees.

Once KBAA began hiring this way, it didn't take long for these ambitious newcomers to start asking how they could move up in the organization. These fresh-out-of-school people wanted to know how to get an "A"! So KBAA developed career paths. The paths were outlined in a formal document—a PowerPoint slide deck—with the positions an associate art consultant can aspire to within the organization, and the skills they need to master at each level to be considered for a promotion.

In the years since KBAA created its first purposeful career paths, the company has expanded them to include both high-potential employees on a management track and high-potential employees who want to get into non-management roles in sales or the creative side of the business. Providing

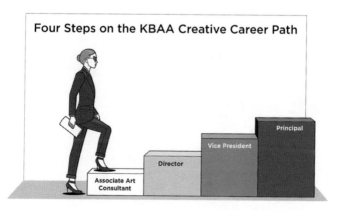

Four Steps on the KBAA Creative Career Path

Associate Art Consultant

Director

Vice President

Principal

people with alternative career paths helped these high-potentials follow their passion, and helped KBAA retain the talent that fueled the company's growth. One high-potential employee was hired as a generalist but chose to move toward the creative side of the business and now works as an art director where she manages a creative team. Two other high-potentials who were hired as generalists have become top salespeople.

The strategy of delegation

Establishing career paths lets high-potential employees know what skills they'll need to acquire to grow inside the company. Strategic delegation is a way they will learn those skills.

Strategic delegation means assigning tasks in a deliberate way to help people gain the knowledge or experience they need to take over for someone higher up in the company. Some companies call

FOLLOW THE TRAIL ▶ KBAA'S CAREER PATHS

KBAA's career paths have kept high-potential employees challenged and looking forward to their futures with the company — helping KBAA grow stronger. Check out KBAA's original career paths—outlined in a PowerPoint slide deck.

this progression planning or experiential learning. Whatever it's called, it should be an integral part of professional development.

If you're a manager, you can train a high-potential direct report on responsibilities associated with your position, one task at a time. Then, when you are promoted, that person will be ready to do your job. If you haven't trained someone, you may find yourself stuck, along with everyone who reports to you.

When strategic delegation works well, everyone does some tasks above their pay grade until the company is ready to add a position. Then the promotions begin to flow. Work moves up and back between levels as people shift roles. It looks like this:

Work Moves Up and Back Between Levels

When strategic delegation works well, everyone does some tasks above their pay grade until the company is ready to add a position. Then the promotions begin to flow.

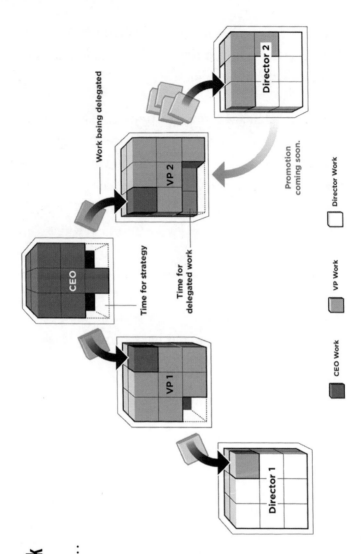

Remember HdL? In 2010, Andy Nickerson was running the client services team for the revenue, audit, and operations company. He also was in line to succeed the company's founder as CEO. That happened the following year. But even after stepping into his new role, Nickerson continued to run client services. Needless to say, it was a lot, and not ideal for either Nickerson or HdL.

A few years later, Nickerson hired Bobby Young as a principal in the client services department. Pretty quickly, Nickerson realized that Young was a high-potential employee who could be developed to lead the department. So, little by little, delegating strategically, Nickerson helped Young learn the job. And while, on paper, Nickerson continued to manage client services, Young effectively took over more and more of those tasks. In 2018, Young was formally promoted to the title of director of client services. Nobody was happier than Nickerson.

As the example shows, high-potentials should get more work because they have the talent (and drive) to *do* more work and accept more responsibilities. To avoid overburdening them, leaders should delegate work broadly among their direct reports—ideally, mostly high-potentials. And those direct reports also should delegate, with tasks and responsibilities cascading down and through the company org chart. In this way, the larger workforce becomes a growing, dynamic talent pool ready to take on new challenges.

In the course of these strategic delegations and shifting responsibilities, you may become aware of employees you hadn't initially spotted as high-potentials because they will see what's going on around them and ask for opportunities to do higher-level work. And you may discover that people you thought were high-potentials are really high-performers content to stay in their lane and not assume more diverse responsibilities. This is all good because it helps you better align opportunity with those who seek it and can deliver.

How strategic delegation supports succession planning

If the entire company successfully practices strategic delegation, everyone will be capable of moving up the organizational chart when they are needed. Another name for that is succession planning.

When leaders talk about needing to do succession planning, what they're really thinking about is who on the team could do their job if they suddenly weren't around for one reason or another. The next step is creating a career path for those potential

VIDEO ▶ STRATEGIC DELEGATION IN ACTION

Watch this animation demonstrating the cascading flow of work between levels when strategic delegation is done right.

successors, and then delegating tasks to them in a strategic way so they learn how to do those things at a reasonable pace.

The ultimate goal is to have enough high-potential people doing better work at a higher level and itching for new challenges. That drives growth.

To see the power of succession planning, let's pay a visit to Arborwell, a midsized California company that provides arborist services for apartment complexes, homeowners' associations, golf courses, and other commercial clients. Since it started in 2001, the company has expanded to 190 employees and six locations up and down the West Coast.

Arborwell couldn't have grown the way it did if Peter Sortwell, the company's founder and CEO, had not hired Andy Lavelle as an operations manager. In his first job interview, Lavelle said his goal was to take over from Sortwell one day. "Although I liked the answer, I was shocked," Sortwell says. He also says that he knew the day would come when he'd need someone to take over as president in order for the company to continue to grow.

So, Sortwell created an ad hoc succession plan. Although Lavelle excelled in some areas, such as working in the field, he was weaker in others, such as customer interactions. Sortwell mentored him. "He did everything I asked of him and did it consistently," Sortwell says. "Consistency is one of those things you see in a person that's going to be successful." Eventually, Lavelle was promoted to chief operations officer. And, in 2013, eight years after joining the company, he succeeded Sortwell as president.

Training and mentoring: Growth accelerators

Americans love stories about self-made men and women. Pride in our ability to figure things out and go it alone looms large in our national mythos.

Lucky for us, many midsized company owners and CEOs know that's not how things really work in business. They're happy to work with individuals and teams, sharing their past successes and failures—just as Arborwell's CEO shared what he'd learned over the years with the person who succeeded him. They don't expect anyone—even their high-potentials—to figure everything out themselves, on their own. They know that by passing on their learned experiences they're growing tomorrow's leaders and ensuring the futures of their organizations.

This type of knowledge transfer is what internal training and mentoring is all about. By sharing large amounts of their wisdom in small amounts of time, senior leaders can help high-potential employees develop much faster, magnifying their impact.

Mentorships are one way to teach people how to do a specific job as a part of a career path. But they're more than that. They can help high-potentials internalize a company's mission and values, its standing in the industry, its customers and marketing philosophy. Mentors can pass on gems that generally don't make it into the employee manual: how clients or coworkers prefer to communicate, or how to approach the most exacting C-suite executives.

MBH Architects is an architectural and interior design firm with offices in New York City, Denver, the San Francisco Bay Area, and Mumbai. Employees who start out as designers can work their way up to job captains and eventually project managers. But there's a lot to learn about architecture's nuts and bolts in that middle level that could stop high-potential employees from advancing.

A few years ago, MBH started a mentorship program for mid-level high-potential employees to learn those key skills. A project manager who was a technical whiz was interested in sharing what he knew. He

IN DEPTH ▶ THE ARBORWELL INTERVIEW

Read another of Arborwell's development success stories: an employee fresh out of college turned director of marketing and business development. Explore the journey and development in the full detailed summary of the interview between the author and CEO Peter Sortwell and the analysis and advice on *Forbes*.

began a "job captain school," training six people at a time in a series of Wednesday afternoon classes that lasted four months. The company has trained eight groups to date and more people want in than there's room for.

Employees in job captain positions who've been through the training "have done a better job," MBH co-founder Dennis Heath says. And a large percentage of them have earned their architect licenses. "The class definitely spurs people to learn more about the field."

Mentoring makes for better employees and improves decision making. It drives innovation, breaks down silos, and creates a stronger connection to an organization's broader vision. It's typical for employees and even managers everywhere, but especially in midsized businesses, to understand their own job or department far better than they do the ins and outs of the entire organization. Because they don't see the big picture, they may be ambivalent

IN DEPTH ▶ THE MBH INTERVIEW

MBH fully committed to the development of their mentorship program, even taking their  best project manager offline to teach the program. Read the full detailed summary of the interview between the author and Founding Principal Dennis Heath and the analysis and advice on *Forbes*.

about collaborating with other departments, or resent them for consuming scarce resources.

Mentoring is a lens through which people can see the connections that exist between departments, and why it's in everyone's best interest to work together. This is especially true when the employee is mentored by a senior leader from another department who can share a perspective that the employee may not be accustomed to hearing.

How to create mentorship programs

Mentoring plays a key role in high-potential employees' career paths and professional development. But creating a mentorship program doesn't need to be complicated, at least not at the start.

Trihydro, an environmental engineering firm headquartered in Laramie, Wyoming, created a mentor program in 2015 that's been crucial to its growth. The program started with a short bulleted list of action steps:

- Pick someone to lead the program.

- Identify potential high-potential employees to include.

- Encourage mentors to participate.

- Make goals clear.

- Match proteges to mentors.

- Set expectations.

- Schedule regular check-ins.

- If it takes off, consider providing nominal training for mentors and mentees.

Over the course of several discussions with Kurt Tuggle, then a Trihydro business unit manager, Emily Bauder, then a Trihydro project staff engineer, came up with the idea to use mentoring to help preserve institutional knowledge before the company's senior employees retired—a problem many companies are facing today as the Baby Boom generation exits the stage. Management loved the idea and put her in charge of developing the program in coordination with Tuggle. Since then, Trihydro has expanded mentoring to keep high-potential employees on the payroll longer, and help new hires assimilate Trihydro's culture.

It was clear from the start that people were hungry to learn. When Bauder kicked off the program in 2015, 97 of Trihydro's 350 employees signed up for mentoring. By 2020, the company had 475 employees, and 128 mentor-mentee pairs, all of whom were matched based on their responses to an in-house survey.

Mentorships at Trihydro aren't always between senior- and junior-level people. "We do a lot of similar level pairing," Bauder says. "We had a lot of individuals join the company in 2019, so we paired people across offices to help them understand how people in their same position do things, and how to do things the Trihydro way."

Tuggle, now Trihydro's President and CEO, is proud of how the mentoring program has enabled knowledge sharing between employees. "As you might expect, those people tend to grow faster within the company than the average employee," Tuggle says.

And it's cost effective. According to Bauder, "If we can retain one employee each year because they've been empowered or learned more, or we've increased their ability to do their job better, we've basically paid for the program."

The payoff for mentoring high-potential employees

Trihydro's mentoring program may be larger than what most midsized companies will contemplate. But mentoring needn't be organized on such a grand scale. However many employees are mentored, that

IN DEPTH ▶ THE TRIHYDRO INTERVIEW

Dive deeper into Trihydro's successful mentorship program: check out Trihydro's Career Planning Template and Mentoring Plan Template and read the full detailed summary of the interview between the author and CEO Kurt Tuggle and the analysis and advice on *Forbes*.

alone can spur growth in high-potential employees and benefit the business.

Arborwell, the California company that provides arborist services, shows the outsized effects of small-scale mentoring of a high-potential employee.

Peter Sortwell, Arborwell's CEO, personally mentored Kimberly Taylor, then a new college graduate who'd joined the company as an entry-level marketing associate. Sortwell invited her to attend association meetings, introduced her to vendors, supported her in taking marketing classes. When Sortwell was invited to speak at industry events, he often sent her instead. Taylor proved to be such a proficient networker and public speaker, she switched her career path from marketing to sales, helping Arborwell cement relationships with customers. She also joined the board of a local real estate association, and subsequently served as its president.

When Arborwell opened an office in Seattle, Taylor used her networking skills and connections within the real estate association to meet members of the group's chapter in that city. That gave her an in to learn more about the Seattle market, which ultimately helped the company land business.

Taylor spent nine years at Arborwell before leaving for a new opportunity. Sortwell says the time and energy he invested in advancing her career paid off handsomely. "She did wonders for the company because she ended up being a sort of spokesperson," he says. "She was out there in the marketplace, socializing with lots of people. She was just a great networker. She opened doors wherever we went because she had that type of personality." All of that was great for Arborwell's business.

Before I leave the subject, it's worth noting that mentoring is different from coaching. Mentors pass on their experience; coaches help people sort through their problems. Coaches may not share the same background as the employees they work with. Instead, they guide people using the Socratic method, asking questions in a way that gets people thinking more deeply and effectively in order to solve their own problems. Midsized companies are unlikely to have separate mentoring and coaching programs. If they have anything, it's likely to include a combination of both.

Leadership programs

Mentoring helps midsized companies pass down often uncodified institutional knowledge to high-potential employees. The examples I've shared illustrate what a powerful growth accelerator it can be. The flip side of in-house professional development is providing high-potential employees with resources from outside the organization—classes, peer groups, leadership development programs, and coaches.

Although high-potential employees at all levels can benefit from external resources, for the purposes of this discussion I'm going to focus on opportunities for high-potentials who've been identified as having what it takes to be a leader.

My heart and work are with this group. At Mastering Midsized, we teach people to be better managers and leaders. We have deep experience in building up leaders, and midsized companies need more of them. It's not hard to find craft-based training in sales, marketing, supply chain, or practically every other professional or business function. Finding leadership development that fits your circumstances and needs is not so easy.

Choosing the right leadership development program

Midsized companies have several leadership-development formats to choose from for management-track high-potential employees. These include external training, peer groups, emerging leader programs, and individual coaching. Many are not that expensive. Let's take a look at each.

External training. As high-potential employees move through their career paths, they may need to hone specific skills in order to advance. That presents a perfect opportunity for external training—something midsized companies don't do often enough. But if people haven't mastered the basics, you're wasting your money and their time. Getting them trained on the basics could be as simple as recommending a book on leadership, or a class or YouTube video on Excel, Word, the CRM, or other software applications they use at work.

You'll find plenty of leadership courses on popular training platforms such as LinkedIn Learning. If your company has a learning management system (LMS), you could buy a module that high-potential employees on a leadership track can work through at their own pace, or as a group. If you find that people ask questions about the same issues over and over—how to manage a new sales rep, for example—it could be a signal that you should record your own short lessons on the solution and upload them to the LMS.

Peer groups. Peer groups exist across industries, by job function, for professions, and around common subjects such as government regulation. As with mentoring, high-potential leaders can benefit from peer groups by learning from others' experiences faster than they could on their own.

Peer groups are especially helpful for high-potential leaders who've been at the same company for some time and need to understand how other smart leaders work and think. Peer groups enable this. The company gains by helping its high-potentials broaden their knowledge base—all for the price of a membership.

Company presidents or CEOs also can benefit from peer groups. If leaders don't continue to develop themselves professionally, they can fall behind. If that happens, and they don't own the business, they eventually will have to answer to the person who does. And even owners are usually accountable to someone, whether it's a board, family, or investors.

Groups such as the Young Presidents Organization can support top leaders. Vistage, a group for CEOs and key executives, is well known, and I speak frequently at their meetings. I've personally benefited from being part of the Alliance of Chief Executives, a regional group for key executives based in northern California.

Emerging leader programs. High-potential employees who are on track to become company leaders may benefit from development over and above what mentoring, outside standard training, or peer groups can provide. One approach that we've found successful is to create customized development programs blending content, discussion and related coaching that makes a client's leadership team far more ready for succession and growth.

The content of these programs can cover all aspects of business, including dealing with current company challenges. The format of group sessions may be as simple as meeting every month for 90 minutes to discuss a business book everyone's read, and how to act on ideas pulled from it. Or, a group could meet more often, over weekly coffee or Zoom calls.

Koshland Pharm, a Bay Area compounding pharmacy, runs emerging leader programs for a handful of high-potential employees who were promoted into middle-manager positions without previous management experience. Megan Patton, a principal in our firm, runs a monthly session with this group. In it, the group discusses takeaways from a management or leadership book. She also has monthly meetings with each group member, and quarterly check-ins with CEO Peter Koshland.

Megan's work takes away some of the training burden from the CEO, who founded the firm and is a self-taught manager. "I don't have an MBA," Koshland says. "Our managers really needed some clear mentorship around making that transition from worker to manager."

The trainings have helped managers solve issues they previously weren't equipped to handle. For example, Jeremy, a manager who oversees a large production crew, struggled to get staff to share feedback during monthly all-hands meetings. Megan suggested he give conversation prompts to his team ahead of meetings—simple questions like asking what they did over the weekend or if they have pets or kids— so they had time to think through their responses, and so Jeremy could call on people directly without having them feel off guard. Her suggestion opened such a floodgate of suggestions from the rest of the group that there now isn't enough time in meetings to hear from everyone.

The feedback from managers who've taken part has been universally positive, Koshland says. "They look forward to their meetings."

Stan Schneider, CEO at Real-Time Innovations (RTI), has trained emerging leaders for more than 20 years. Schneider hit on the idea during the dot-com boom, when the company, which makes software that allows other applications to share information in real time, grew from six people to 60 in 18 months. Of those employees, 40 were engineers from Stanford University. But none were managers. Schneider put together a half dozen classes that covered leadership, time management, personal growth, teamwork, and communications. Classes met every other week, with discussions and, yes, homework.

Flash forward to present day. Six people from Schneider's original training class of ten are still in management roles. The program has been so successful that today all new employees take part. The training now includes modules designed specifically for managers and future managers. There are others about basic corporate operations and more general skills. "I love teaching it, that's part of the reason I do it," Schneider says.

CEOs rarely have the time or temperament to handle this kind of training on their own. But it gives you an idea of what's possible, even if you opt to hire someone to do the work.

Individual coaching. Thousands of articles and books address professional development, but providing high-potential employees with access to professional coaching speeds up the process. Coaches combine their own experience with their coaching skills—what they've read plus what they've learned from experience and their other clients. As they learn about your high-potential employees' circumstances, they can figure out what an individual needs and can benefit from by accessing their internal database of relevant material. For the employee, and for your business, that's not just efficient, it can be a pearl beyond price.

If you're looking for a coach, be clear on your purpose:

- Do you need someone who can coach a high-potential on fundamental management skills?

- Is improving interpersonal skills a key part of the work?

- How closely should the coach's past experience match what is needed?

- Is teaching a high-potential how to process and reflect the priority?

Whatever the need is, there must be a comfortable fit between coach and student. And coaching is not like psychoanalysis; it isn't meant to last forever. Review how people have progressed every six months to make sure you and your high-potential are still getting a return on investment.

For example, OBMI, a hospitality design firm headquartered in Miami with offices in Texas, the Middle East, and the Caribbean islands, launched a one-year leadership development program with Mastering Midsized as part of its succession planning process. The goal of the program is to develop both new leaders and high-potential performers who are expected to step into upper-level management when present leaders retire. Led by Megan Patton, the program consists of monthly group discussions of material that participants read in advance, plus one-on-one sessions. The curriculum covers standard management topics such as teamwork, talking to employees, and creating career paths for direct reports. As part of the program, we also check in

IN DEPTH ▶ THE RTI INTERVIEW

RTI's training program includes classes on over 20 topics and is open to managers and employees alike. Explore some of the topics

 and RTI's theory on all-level inclusive training in the full detailed summary of the interview between the author and CEO Stan Schneider and the analysis and advice on *Forbes*.

quarterly with the manager to ensure development is on track. This, as we'll see, is critical.

Assessing leaders

Mentoring, training programs, coaching, peer groups, and other internal and external professional development tools can help high-potential employees advance as leaders. But it's not enough to implement these programs, you must track them. To do that, you need to establish a baseline assessment of where your leaders are now. Only then can you measure how they are developing and growing.

Unfortunately, most midsized firms don't have an effective process for evaluating development. Far too often when high-performers are delegated harder work, or take on other development or learning opportunities, the company doesn't check to see if they've learned, what they've learned, or whether they've improved.

Why? Because evaluating people is uncomfortable. Most midsized companies have neither a process for making assessments, nor anyone to run it. Emerging midsized companies may have a single HR generalist on staff and no budget for a learning and development specialist to help with reviews.

Fortunately, the solution isn't complicated. The best tool for determining how a high-potential is performing is a regular performance review. While that sounds like common sense, midsized companies don't do performance reviews often enough or well enough.

Before deciding when or how to do them, you must pick out the learning and development objectives upon which to base your reviews. For that, you need a rubric, which is a set of criteria to determine how well high-potential employees are measuring up to expectations. Once you've identified and clarified the objectives, there are a couple options for assessing the results, including traditional performance reviews and 360s.

A rubric for evaluation

A prerequisite of learning and development is selecting the new capabilities a high-potential employee needs to develop. Should they learn to lead through influence rather than control on large cross-functional projects? Should they work on improving their technical strengths or their interpersonal skills? Once you determine the goals, you need to create a map that charts their progress toward achieving them. A rubric for evaluating someone's performance does that.

This rubric that we helped develop for a real estate development leader is an example of what this type of evaluation tool can cover:

1.   An entrepreneurial eye for opportunity.

2. The ability to manage and motivate a team.

3. Thinks like an investment strategist, able to analyze and understand complex financial arrangements.

4. Detailed understanding of the qualified application process for financing.

5. Able to analyze site, zoning, traffic, and construction constraints.

6. Make judgment calls on risk taking and risk mitigation.

7. Strong cross-disciplinarity decision maker.

8. Outgoing, relationship oriented toward internal team, consultants, and internal and external partners.

A rubric helps a manager evaluate high-potential employees' performance in segments, identifying areas of strength as well as areas needing improvement. It also helps maximize their contribution to the organization, while matching them to positions which they'll enjoy and in which they'll perform well.

Performance reviews—How they can make a difference

Performance reviews are the heart of assessing leaders. When reviewing high-potential leaders, use a pre-defined rubric. But for the best outcome, take the following factors into consideration as well:

- **Spend more time talking about the future than the present.** In a review, confirm that a high-potential leader is delivering on the core duties of the job. But spend the bulk of the time reviewing the progress they're making on their development path. Although it's important to look at the present, it's even more important to help a high-potential employee understand what they need to do to thrive in the future—your company depends on it.

- **Be honest.** Going easy on a high-potential leader isn't kind. It keeps them in the dark. The best way to be kind is to be honest so they can improve and grow.

- **Congratulate and recognize strengths.** Validating success is food for the soul for high-potential leaders. Congratulations don't have to be elaborate. They can take the form of positive comments on an achievement, or praise for a win. Always emphasize positives over negatives. And spread the word to others. Another way to congratulate high-potentials is to give them more challenging work that prepares them for their next promotion.

- **Deliver feedback on a regular basis.** Every quarter or six months is a good frequency. I'm not a fan of "continuous performance reviews" because, in practice, "continuous" usually means they never happen.

- **Lend a hand in areas where they need it.** Hey, developing new capabilities is hard, and the path is marked by frequent failures. Remember: People learn from failure, especially when mentors and managers are standing by to help them put it in context and pick up the pieces.

No need to lead with your eyes closed: Use 360s

In 360-degree performance reviews, or 360s, superiors, peers, and subordinates anonymously share how an employee is performing, based on their interactions with the person.

Typically, a coach compiles the results and shares them with the employee. The intention is to understand how others see the person compared to how they see themselves, shedding light on blind spots. The best 360s benchmark the leader being reviewed against national results for other leaders. 360s can focus on behavior, but also on expertise, teamwork, and more.

Fundamentally, people love to follow great leaders. But the only way really to know how much people enjoy following you is to ask them. While the accomplishment of tasks and goals is one element of success for a leader, another is your impact on others. Periodic 360s measure a leader's development over time and can identify where someone is succeeding and where they need to improve.

One of our clients learned that lesson when they contacted us for help. A senior leader there wanted to help a middle manager who had been twice passed up for promotion. The manager was talented but determined and would become a flight risk if his career path had ended. He was dedicated and smart, but "had sharp elbows," tough on anyone who didn't spend as much time as he did at his desk, cranking out work.

The client hired us to take the manager through some one-on-one coaching. Our consultant did a 360 review at the beginning of her work with the manager. It showed that other employees saw him quite differently than the manager saw himself; there were dangerous blind spots. He overused the commanding style and underused the energizing and affirming style. And, clearly, it was a surprise to him. The review hit him hard, but he accepted it. And he dedicated himself to changing how he interacted and led. For one, he spent more time connecting with people on his team, which built trust.

A year later, when the coach finished coaching the manager, she conducted another 360. The difference was obvious. His was spending more time relating to others and doing so more effectively. Those sharp elbows had been smoothed down. And how he saw himself now lined up with how others saw him. The blind spots were gone. And the next time the manager was up for a promotion, he got it.

Coaching works. It just does.

You don't need a dedicated HR person to do this, and it's unlikely your first HR hire would be an expert in learning and developing. If you begin by focusing, as I've advised, on a relatively small group of high-potentials, a small amount of your executives' time should do the trick, especially if you follow the guidelines we've outlined above. If it would help, hire an outside coach for a few hours a month to provide support. That's easy, not terrifically expensive, and well worth it.

Hire for potential, not just performance

It's not enough to hire high-performers who, at their peak, can just do the job you hired them to do. They may do that job very, very well. But that's not always enough.

Midsized companies must hire for tomorrow's jobs and needs. They require people with raw skills and experience, who, with development, can become the leaders and star performers the organization will need in the future. These companies need people who want more responsibility and will move up in the organization. People drive growth!

When you're recruiting, some new hires should come from the high-potential talent pool. High-potential employees may cost more, but they tend to be worth more in the long run (presuming you're interested in the long run).

Say you're filling a position for an accounting clerk. You'll pay more for an accounting graduate with a few years of work experience who is looking for advancement than for a career bookkeeper with more experience but no degree. It's worth it to pay for and develop the graduate not because he or she can do the job you hire them for but *for what they can become.* Their knowledge of accounting concepts should help them rise through the ranks to become your accountant in three years, and your controller in five or 10.

I don't suggest that midsized companies hire overqualified people all the time. But when you find people who can combine their smarts and behavioral characteristics with the experience they'll gain working for you, it will position them to be promoted. With enough of those hires, you'll have a pipeline of great talent. Fail to do this, and you'll always be

THE POWER OF 360S

360 reviews can be powerful change agents, offering leaders the gift of seeing how others see them and coming face to face with their leadership brand. Read a real-world example of a 360-degree review in action in this *Forbes* article.

heading out to the job market, making risky and ultimately more expensive hires. You may have many high-performers, but that's not the same as having a pool of high-potentials primed for promotion.

Developing high-potentials pays big dividends

Professional development helps midsized companies cultivate smart, capable people who are ready and able to step up. Yes, it's great to keep high achievers engaged and happy. And high-potential people thrive working for a challenging and rewarding employer. But the reason you're doing all this is to make sure the company achieves its goals.

So, maintain a high level of development every month of every quarter of every year. Keep your high-potentials excited about the next skill they can learn and master. Make continuous development an explicit promise and create a plan for how to do it. Give these high-potentials what they crave. This is not an HR policy; it is a business growth plan.

MORE PROFESSIONAL DEVELOPMENT READING

We've studied the subject of professional development in emerging midsized companies for some time. If you want to dive in more, scan the QR code for more articles and research, assessments, and other assistance.

MORE COPIES OF THIS BOOK?

Does someone you know need to read this chapter? Of course, you can order a book for  them online, but if they're out of stock, or you need quantities, want to drop ship to many different locations, or this is related to a peer group or speaking event, scan this code.

WANT *TO TALK* ABOUT PROFESSIONAL DEVELOPMENT?

Mastering Midsized provides support and guidance for midsized companies who need to improve their professional development. Scan this QR code for the fastest route to talk to someone about getting help.

AUDIO DOWNLOAD OF CHAPTER 3

Listen to author Robert Sher read this chapter. Scan this QR code to instantly download and play on your device.

CHAPTER 3

The Journey from "I" to "We" Leadership

I f small company founders or CEOs want their businesses to reach midsized status, they'll need help. They can't do it by themselves. That's just not the way it works. Having a single inspired leader may work for a startup or a small business. It may even work for companies at the low end of the $10 million to $1 billion revenue range of midsized companies. But to tackle more complex issues, to take advantage of opportunities that arise as a business scales, midsized companies need a team of strong leaders.

And that's the third key people driver that helps midsized companies accelerate their growth: adopting a team-based leadership model.

To grow, midsized companies must transition from what's commonly referred to as the hub-and-spoke model, in which the CEO gives orders and everyone else salutes and executes. In a team leadership model, the CEO works with a leadership team to develop a plan, together, and then provides direction and oversight, leaving it to the team and their direct reports to hammer out the details.

When this model is firing on all cylinders, teams are cohesive. Members trust and talk to each other. Each leader has a role, but they coordinate, think, and work together toward a common goal. As various organizational leaders assume more responsibilities for day-to-day operational tasks, the CEO and the top leadership team spend more time looking at the big picture, strategizing for the future. That's when growth begins. And that's an inspiring thing to see.

Advice Media wouldn't be the company it is today if CEO Shawn Miele hadn't switched from calling all the shots to sharing decision-making and strategic planning with his top leadership team.

Miele started the Park City, Utah, company in 1998 as a health-care information provider and discussion board. Over the years, he pivoted to building websites and doing search engine optimization (SEO) for health-care providers. But as costs associated with web development and SEO fell, competition increased, and Advice's margins got squeezed. By 2016, even though the company had made acquisitions to grow, another pivot was in order.

Miele is the first to admit that running teams wasn't his forte. At first, his idea of running the business was to make decisions, tell other people how to carry them out, and then go back to his desk, put his head down, and grind. He expected other top company leaders to do the same. "Teamwork is something we struggled with," he says. "We needed individuals who would run with things without consulting with other people." As the company grew and the business became more complex, Miele's leadership style and decision-making process became more and more problematic.

Miele belonged to a peer-mentoring group—like the ones I discussed in the last chapter—and through it took a personality test. It confirmed his gut instinct that his propensity for avoiding delegating decision-making was hurting the business. That was a wake-up call.

One of the first things Miele did was tap his top lieutenants to help him come up with a new strategic plan. Asking for his top leaders' input allowed Miele to profit from what they knew and it made them feel invested in the change. That kind of teamwork—starting at the top level and expanding through the whole organizational chart—eventually became a core company value.

Miele made other changes to embrace a team leadership model, including taking a more systematic approach to hiring, one that included identifying candidates for leadership positions who could be team players. He hired the company's first HR leader to oversee hiring and made sure the managers doing the hiring asked candidates questions that spoke to leadership skills. Miele started holding monthly town hall meetings to talk about the company's mission and values, highlighting the importance of teamwork.

The strategic plan that the top leaders came up with had the immediate effect of steering the company's business away from digital-marketing agency work and toward selling software, including applications for social media marketing, reputation management, and other forms of digital marketing. Expanding the product base increased revenue. That expanded the budget for adding positions, provided leaders with more responsibilities and more opportunities to use strategic delegation to develop junior employees. All this created a cycle of growth.

Since changing its leadership model, Advice Media has more than doubled its annual revenue, from $8 million in 2016 to $20 million in 2020. The company has opened satellite offices in Colorado and New York, and its workforce has grown from about 30 or 40 to 130.

None of it would have happened if Miele hadn't downshifted from hub-and-spoke and revved up to team-led model.

What this chapter covers

Advice Media is hardly alone in its ambition to turn a small business with a small-business leadership style into a midsized company with a more sophisticated approach.

It's a journey every midsized business must make if they want to sustain predictable, systematic growth. In this chapter, I go into more depth about what team leadership looks like, and why it's so important for midsized companies to adopt it, especially if growth is the goal.

I also walk you through the elements that companies need to have in place for a team-leadership model to function as it should. These include a concise business plan, a top leader willing to work in a new, more collaborative way, and other leaders with the right skills to work as a cohesive unit. I'll briefly revisit the subject of strategic delegation that I covered in Chapter 2 to explain how you can use it to develop the team leaders you need to help your company grow.

IN DEPTH ▶ THE ADVICE MEDIA INTERVIEW

Advice Media's journey to develop a team-oriented culture paid off—with a doubling of their revenue, huge expansion, and a strong, cohesive leadership team. Read the full detailed summary of the interview between the author and CEO Shawn Miele and the analysis and advice on *Forbes*.

Philosophy: To sustain growth, midsized companies must adopt a team-based approach to leadership

The kind of hub-and-spoke leadership model that Advice Media once had is common but not adequate for small or midsized companies that want to grow.

Small Business Hub and Spokes Model

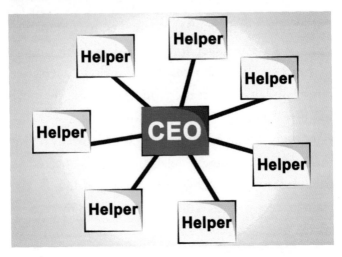

As the CEO gets more and more helpers, they can become overwhelmed and become the bottleneck.

Small businesses and startups often run quite efficiently with a single smart, visionary leader who acts as a hub, with a staff of helpers acting as spokes. The consolidation of decision-making in this model allows small company leaders to be flexible and nimble—just what you need when you're starting out. When you're small, business-building is conducted on a relatively small scale. Building out a customer-service function in a two-person department may mean having one person answer all incoming calls and passing angry customers on to the person who's better at dealing with them. That's a decision you don't need a team of leaders to plan or implement.

But if the CEOs is the only person empowered to make decisions, he or she won't have time to assess and act on opportunities that come up in new markets, or with new customers. While those decisions wait for the CEO to come up for air, direct reports are stuck waiting for orders while they watch opportunities slip away. That's a good way to kill growth. Or problems crop up that are beyond the scope of what a direct report can handle. Then that gets added to the to-dos on the desk of the CEO, who has to scramble and respond in a panic. That is another good way to kill growth.

Once these situations begin to crop up, leaders don't need more helpers; they need a team of leaders who can work with them to assess problems and opportunities and make decisions even when the top leader is absent from the mix. The leadership team is connected to the CEO and each other by a clear plan. Everyone is committed to the plan, and to the other team members. When this connection is present, the leader serves as a coach and co-author of the business plan, and the ultimate source of approval and accountability.

Leading with Teams Takes Hold

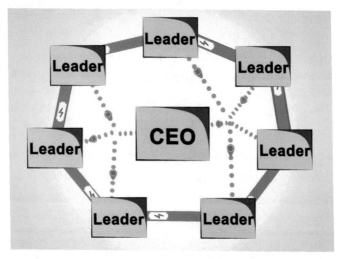

Far less communication must go through the CEO. They are freed up to add value to the business strategically.

Comparing Leadership Models

Dimensions of comparison	Hub-and-Spoke Model	Team Leadership Model
Where decisions are made	CEO	CEO and their leadership team
Direction of input	Top down	Plan-based and multidirectional
CEO mindset	"I know best"	"We know best"
Recruiting approach	Hire helpers to take orders	Hire leaders who figure out how to solve problems
Loyalty	To the CEO	To the mission and vision for the business
Support	Help the CEO	Help other team members get results

Companies are significantly different in six key areas once they transition from the Hub-And-Spoke model.

Team-based leadership is foundational to the growth of midsized companies. I know because in our consulting practice, we work with owners, CEOs, and other top leaders at companies transitioning from hub-and-spoke.

At every stage of a midsized company's growth, the top leader has to focus on the future. At the start of the change from small business to midsized, the future may be just thinking 24 hours ahead and, hard as that sometimes is, it's possible for one person to do it. But to plan for the next year or two, a leader will have to rely on their teams to run the day-to-day and month-to-month aspects of the business. That's another reason why leaders of midsized companies have to ditch the hub-and-spoke model. Sticking with it turns them into chokepoints for decisions on business operations.

I've chosen to focus on the CEO's role in making this arduous journey from hub-and-spoke to team leadership because it is so critical. Although I use "CEO" in this context, I'm also referring to founders, owners, and other top leaders, regardless of title.

As midsized companies pass roughly $75 million in revenue, their top leaders in each business function will have to make the same journey. That won't be easy because it means changing how they view the business, their role in it, and everyone around them. That's a lot. But the larger the company, the more leaders have come to appreciate the advantages of moving from the hub-and-spoke model to team-based leadership, beginning at a higher level and working their way down the organization chart. But making the move is harder than most people think. That's why I'm focusing on how to manage the transition rather than discussing teamwork in general.

So, what could go wrong?

Advice Media faced many of the obstacles that other emerging midsized companies encounter as they make the transition to a team leadership model. But there are more. Other challenges I've encountered in our client work include:

- **The micromanaging CEO.** If the top leader is constantly peering over her direct reports' shoulders or second-guessing them, those reports will find it hard to do their jobs, much less look to assume more responsibilities. People who want (and have the capacity) to lead don't want to be treated like children.

VIDEO ▶ THE POWER OF TEAM-BASED LEADERSHIP

Watch this video demonstrating the hub-and-spoke model vs the team-leadership model and why team-based leadership is foundational to the growth of midsized companies.

- **The laissez-faire CEO.** In other cases, top leaders play everything by the seat of their pants. Their plans are fluid, non-existent, or made on the fly. When this is the case, lower-level leaders may grow frustrated, feeling mistrusted and disrespected because they have little input. This could cause them to underperform and, if their situation doesn't improve, look for greener (and more predictable) pastures.

- **The disengaged CEO.** Sometimes a top leader is so overwhelmed by the demands of the job, he or she opts out—whether they know it or not. I've seen CEOs just stop working, taking (in effect) sabbaticals without providing their direct reports any guidance, letting the chips fall where they may. But people who are accustomed to being told what to do—even people in leadership positions—can't just flip the switch and start making critical, strategic decisions by themselves. Situations like this usually don't end well. And, ultimately, after the chips fall helter-skelter, and the business suffers, the leader's belief that he is indispensable is reinforced.

This happened with one founder-CEO I know. Over seven years, his company had ballooned to more than 120 employees. He knew in his gut that he was a better entrepreneur than a corporate manager. And he knew that a company that had reached the size his had could benefit from a more systematic approach to leadership, something an experienced corporate manager could offer. That was smart and intuitive. So, he hired a professional CEO. Then the founder checked out for a six-month sabbatical to recharge his batteries without laying out a plan that the new CEO and the leadership team could execute. That wasn't so smart. When he returned, the business was headed in a direction he didn't like. He fired the new CEO and took back the reins. He still needed an experienced corporate manager, but he no longer thought that was the answer to his problems. He was wrong, and ultimately sold his business for far less than he had planned.

- **The wrong people in team leader roles.** CEOs may not have the right people on staff to implement a team-leadership model and end up delegating tasks to reports who lack the skills, experience, or team mindset for the roles they are being asked to play. That could be the consequence of underinvesting in people. Or perhaps someone was promoted into a position on the top leadership team because of his tenure rather than his qualifications. When unqualified leaders fail to deliver, the CEO can start thinking that this team-leadership thing is bunk. Then the business snaps back into the hub-and-spoke model, and its growth is inhibited… perhaps permanently.

- **The team never gels.** Say a CEO manages to get out of the way and delegates responsibilities to next-level leaders. Those individuals could all be high-performers. They may also not get along or work well together. Perhaps one's loud personality grates on quieter members of the team. Narcissists, know-it-alls, and rabid competitors can all undermine a team. Bad group dynamics make it impossible for a team to work cohesively. A misfiring team can force the CEO to mediate constantly, draining the group's morale, wasting time, inviting burn-out, and tempting the CEO to disband the team.

Transitioning to team-based leadership

Midsized companies can bypass these and other problems common to transitioning from a hub-and-spoke to team-based leadership model if they build the following five elements into their approach:

- Designing and writing a business plan and review process

- Vetting leaders for collaborative skills

- A top leader focusing on the future

- Emphasizing collaboration and team cohesion

- Making strategic delegation a core business process

I'll use this section to take a closer look at each.

A written business plan and review process

A clear business plan and a process to review it on a regular basis serve as the foundation of strong leadership teams. You can't just tell leaders what they need to do. For a leadership team to work in a way that moves the company toward shared goals, you must commit those goals to writing. I often say, "If it's not written down, it doesn't exist." And you must create a process to keep the team accountable for meeting the goals you have written.

Formal growth targets correlate to stronger financial performances. A study by Ohio State University and GE Capital of nearly 1,500 midsized companies found that those recording the strongest financial performance were most likely to possess at least the core elements of a business plan.

At Mastering Midsized, we recommend that companies adopt a One Page Business Plan® and review it regularly. A One Page Business Plan® has five elements:

1. A vision describing the future

2. A mission statement clarifying the organization's purpose

3. Objectives defining and quantifying goals

4. Strategies serving as a growth blueprint

5. Action plans spelling out how to implement strategies

Smaller midsized companies can use a single business plan; larger ones may need separate plans for each department.

When crafting a business plan to run your company, remember these key points:

Keep it simple. Include only the most important elements. A list of bullet points is enough.

Be intentional. Each team leader's focus should be clear.

Include goals. All leaders should be able to describe what winning looks like for them: their responsibilities and projects, and key performance indicators (KPIs) they have to meet.

DOWNLOAD A SAMPLE ONE PAGE BUSINESS PLAN®

Keeping your plans clear and concise improves execution and drives results and growth. Download a sample one-page plan here.

Know what matters. Priorities should be clear so there's no question about what is most important to the business. This makes goals achievable. Midsized companies have neither infinite time nor infinite resources. They can't execute every good idea, only the best.

Put it in writing. Business plans should be written, approved by the team, and made easily accessible. It's not enough to discuss goals or save a plan in an email thread. A business plan has to be hashed out, prioritized, recorded, and implemented in an orderly way, with leaders acting as a unit. This way, they can consider all the options, choose the most important to act on, ignore the others, and get down to work.

Review progress once a month. Ask each leader working to a One Page Business Plan® to report on their progress each month and keep a record of their results. If parts of the plan are updated, update the whole plan, in writing. Regularly reviewing and updating the business plan is the only way to manage the urgent but perhaps less important matters that land in your inbox. The very act of making team leaders report on their activity and results reinforces the importance of focusing on the top priorities; if progress toward key goals isn't being made, everyone will know it.

If you've been operating without a business plan, ease into adopting one. At first, top leaders may feel uncomfortable being held accountable to targets and will need time to adjust to new requirements. If team leaders miss targets, they may worry that will make a plan-review meeting tense, or even ugly. In such an atmosphere, morale can sink, and leaders might end up pressuring you to shelve the planning process and go back to the "good old days." You don't want that and it's not likely to happen if you start slowly, letting the process mature, increasing accountability incrementally.

Done correctly, business plans generate cohesion in a leadership team, and serve as a powerful pathway to growth.

For example, the CEO of a family-run wholesale foods distributor approached us for help to increase the company's valuation before the family would decide whether to sell the business. The leaders who reported to him had been with the business for years. Honestly, their work was uninspired, and they didn't operate as an empowered team. That was reflected in the company's sales growth, which was lower than it should have been, and its profits, which were close to zero.

The company had never had a business plan. We worked with them to create seven One Page Business Plans®: one for the company and one each for the six top leaders. The plans outlined a one-year strategy, related projects, and key metrics and established a review schedule. In the course of attending those plan review meetings, department leaders began to talk to each other. They also started to do more problem-solving than they had in the past. They discovered areas they could collaborate on to improve inventory turns, and institute other efficiencies.

Not surprisingly, profits suddenly appeared in that first year. In the second, the leaders' skill at managing to a business plan improved… as, again, did the company's profits. They improved so much that the company could afford to hire a vice president of sales. That led to even higher sales and profits. In the third year of using business plans, the CEO declined a significant offer for the business. Selling was no longer on the table. As time went by, the hits kept coming. After seven years of using business plans, annual sales had nearly tripled from $18 million to $52 million, and pre-tax profits went from almost zilch to a robust 6%.

Another client, Pinchin, a national environmental consulting firm headquartered in Mississauga, Canada, adopted a new business planning process in 2015 as part of upgrading its operational planning systems in the wake of the company founder's death. Over the previous decade, Pinchin had experienced tremendous organic growth—expanding its workforce from 80 to 400 people. The company was also expanding its leadership team. Both solid reasons for adopting a more systematic approach to planning. Approximately

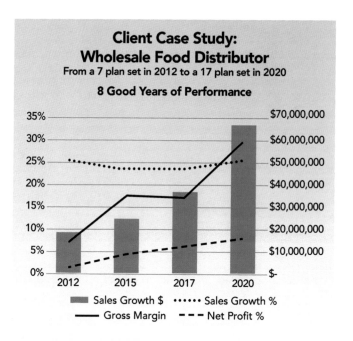

Client Case Study:
Wholesale Food Distributor
From a 7 plan set in 2012 to a 17 plan set in 2020

8 Good Years of Performance

Legend:
- Sales Growth $
- •••••• Sales Growth %
- —— Gross Margin
- – – Net Profit %

50 leaders were brought into the planning process, representing the two levels of leadership below the CEO. Each leader developed a One Page Business Plan®, and all leaders could see all the plans on a company web portal. This transparency helped leaders—and their teams—understand where their work fit into the company's overall strategy. As leaders got comfortable working to plan and with the plan reviews, they completed more initiatives on time.

As Pinchin's leadership grew stronger, it fostered a closer working relationship with Pinchin West, a sister company started by the same founder. Although the companies shared his name, they had long operated as separate entities with their own presidents, boards, and financials. The closer relationship led to working on joint business plans, and that led to a 2017 merger.

Today, the combined organization has a workforce of 800. That size and level of growth couldn't have happened—and certainly not successfully—without the clarity about leadership roles and goals a business plan offers.

So, what can go wrong *now?*

The leaders situation

Creating a clear business plan is the foundation for a successful team-based leadership model. After that concrete is poured, it's time to build teams and the leadership that can deliver results based on the plan.

If your company is changing from a hub-and-spoke model to a team-led approach, you can't just assume that the people stepping into team leader roles will have the appropriate skills to execute on the plan and guide their direct reports. They may. But based on my experience working with leaders of midsized companies, the chance is greater that people will be promoted past their level of competence, often out of a sense of loyalty to long-term employees. If those people can't execute, you can rest assured the plan will fail. You must have people who are ready and hungry to step into team leader roles or hire them. I guarantee that if you move people who are helpers into leader roles without any help or professional development, they'll make some bad decisions and you'll pay the price.

In our practice, we've identified several reasons why long-term employees who a CEO assumes are capable of becoming leaders fail when company's growth reaches a tipping point. I wrote about these in my book *Mighty Midsized Companies*. Since then, I've said it again and again:

- **The problems become more complex.** When small companies become midsized (or midsized companies get bigger), they have more customers to cater to, more employees to manage, more locations to open, and more cash to manage. Put that together and a leader is running a more complicated business. There are simply many more opportunities for leaders to overspend and under-collect, while the business gets targeted by larger competitors.

- **The CEO's direct reports aren't top-level leaders.** People the CEO is counting on as his leadership team still function at the helper level, waiting to be told what to do. Their skills and experience are more likely to be associated with work done at the supervisor or manager level, which I'll explain in a bit.

- **The company's leaders lack more sophisticated skills.** Jim is a great bookkeeper. But the company has grown and what it really needs now is a controller. Unfortunately, Jim never took classes in accounting. Now, Jim is a problem.

- **The team doesn't focus on the long term.** Leaders at startups or early-stage companies focus on short-term activities to ensure that the company survives. But as companies grow, leaders need to spend more time thinking about the future. Some leaders find that harder (and less exciting) than others.

How can growing companies address these problems, making sure that their leaders can in fact lead? In my client work, I suggest doing a fitness assessment of every leader at every level every year. Fitness assessments aren't the same as annual reviews. A fitness assessment evaluates the fit between what that leader is bringing to the table and what the organization likely will need in the future. To do this assessment, the CEO creates a written evaluation of the top leadership team. And those top leaders assess their direct reports. The CFO assesses the leader of the finance team, the head of sales assesses the sales leadership team, and so on across the org chart.

I recommend using these six questions as criteria for determining the fitness of leaders at each level:

- Does the person have the experience, skills, and desire to help pull the company growth to the next level?

- Would I hire the person again for their current position?

- Thinking about what the organizational chart will look like in a couple years, am I eager to see the person's name on it?

- What are the person's strengths as a team leader, and team player?

- Has the person worked at a company with the size and complexity that my company is close to reaching? If they haven't, have they been growing professionally along with it?

- How is the person rated by her peers?

The 360-degree performance reviews I described in Chapter 2 are one way to understand how a team leader's peers and direct reports view them compared to how they see themselves. 360s also can identify gaps in knowledge, behaviors, or group dynamics that a leader can work on to fulfill the responsibilities of their position.

If assessments uncover team leaders who aren't working out or don't fit into your company's future, you have two choices. The first is relatively simple compared to the second: You can find a different spot for them in the organization, or you can let them go. The second option is helping them improve. Sound easy? It's not. This option only works if you feel that the person could make the needed improvements in three to six months. And only if three other factors apply:

- **They're hungry for it.** Rehabilitate underperforming leaders only if you've seen them work hard to develop in the past and only if they're still eager to improve (and understand that they need to). Some people, when told they have to get better at their job, will agree and then fake it. Others will sincerely work at it. In one case I'm familiar with, a production manager wasn't assertive enough to drive needed change on the plant floor. But he knew it, accepted coaching, and became an eager learner, which helped him improve his leadership skills quickly.

- **They're capable.** Desire only gets a person so far. A leader must show they can change to work in the way you need them to work. If they don't, it's not doing anyone a favor to keep them in a leader role, as painful as it may be to tell them that. If they have a great attitude but the ability is not there, point them toward other challenges within the organization that they may be more suited to take on successfully—which is what most people want out of work. One engineering director was so quiet that he failed to lead, and coaching didn't couldn't help him become more assertive. The company moved him to a technical role where he could contribute as an individual. He was a better fit there, and he was happier in his work, too.

- **They want to be mentored.** Mentoring immerses people in a company's values, culture, and ways of doing things. That goes for leaders as well as employees in non-leader roles. If as the CEO you decide an executive team leader is worth investing in, you've got to go all-in on helping them. You may need to do so personally, devoting significant time to it, especially if we're talking about a possible successor. Model the behavior you want to see in them. Don't expect to give directions without allotting time for supervision, and then get mad when the work isn't accomplished the way you want it to be. Provide feedback so your mentee knows what's expected, and how he or she is succeeding. But this will only help if the individual wants it.

Focusing on the future

Think about the types of projects a midsized company might have in the works. Completing a lean-manufacturing initiative in the next quarter. Preparing to seek funding from outside investors in six months. R&D for expanding into a new market next year. Making a key acquisition two years from now. It's hard for a CEO to focus on such long-term strategies if they're also managing day-to-day work.

For a team-leadership model to yield the biggest dividends, an increasing amount of short-term work must take place at lower levels in the organization. If it does, the CEO can spend more time on the future, leaving operational decisions to the top leadership team. And those leaders should delegate more day-to-day work to their direct reports, giving themselves more time to make those big operational decisions.

I realize how hard this is. We routinely see midsized companies' top leaders or entire leadership teams so occupied with fire drills and scrambling they don't have time to think about what lies ahead. They don't have the time to develop plans, and their teams are constantly reacting, reacting, reacting. But the fact remains: To succeed, the CEO and top leaders must shift their time horizon to focus on the longer term. Three to five years out is ideal, though it's usually a stretch to get there.

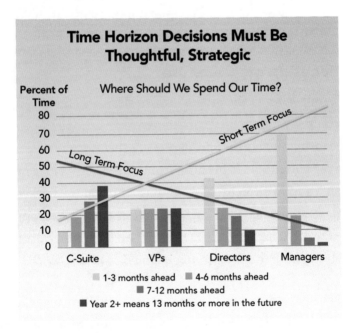

The question becomes, how do you shift your focus to the long term? Based on our client work, here are strategies for making the transition:

- **Force yourself.** If you don't hold yourself to making time for strategic, long-term work, you won't do it. If you're honest with yourself, you know that. Your days and weeks will fill up with short-term, urgent matters, as it always does. Breaking long-term work into smaller more digestible chunks can make such work more tangible and obvious and add clarity to the process of long-term thinking. Creating intermediate deadlines for yourself will give the work an urgency it may otherwise lack. You must commit. You must believe that long-term work is as important, if not more so, than addressing this week's crisis.

- **Strengthen leaders in middle-management roles.** Use professional development to get those leaders prepared to deal with the daily crises that are taking you away from your real job of planning for growth. Improving the middle management cadre may entail replacing weaker middle managers with stronger candidates from either inside or outside the organization.

- **Delegate short-term work.** Trickle projects with shorter timeframes down through the organizational chart to free up time for the top leadership team to do long-term strategic planning.

Here's a hypothetical example of what shifting time horizons can look like. Say an ambitious small company founder wants to cross the $10 million revenue mark in a year, and the $100 million mark in five years. In the beginning, the founder spends at least half her time dealing with day-to-day tasks. As sales take off and the company grows, she can afford to hire a sales manager to run the sales team's day-to-day operations. The founder still spends a lot of time on short-term concerns, but having a sales manager relieves some of that burden.

A year or two goes by and the company has grown a little more. She can now hire a few leaders at the director level. The directors take over more short-term work, and even some longer-term work that's not too far out into the future. At this point, the company has crossed over into midsized territory. In addition to the founder, top-level leaders now include the sales manager—who's been promoted to a director role—as well as a couple of other top leaders.

Because they're all delegating tasks to their direct reports, the top leaders can spend equal amounts of time on projects that cross all points on the company's time scale: short, mid-term, and long. That's as it should be for growing companies. That's particularly as it should be for companies growing quickly.

Think of putting the pedal to the metal when you're driving your car. As you gain speed, you must look further down the road because you're coming up on things more quickly. You have less time to react. It's the same with companies. If you're growing quickly, you'll reach milestones and obstacles sooner than a company that isn't expanding quite so fast. CEOs and their top leadership teams must look further into the future to anticipate and react to what's coming down the road.

Say my hypothetical company has executed so well that its annual revenue has reached the CEO's five-year $100 million goal. That company probably now has four levels of leaders below the founder. The top-level leaders focus pretty much full-time on the future of the company. They create and hand off plans to their vice presidents, and the VPs delegate tasks to their directors, who oversee the managers. And the managers are on the front lines, dealing with day-to-day, short-term work.

How to build good teams

For the workflow that I've just described to operate smoothly, efficiently, and successfully, leaders must work together, and they must work together well. That doesn't happen by chance or accident. Great leadership teams start with people who want to be team players, rather than a bunch of soloists. Getting

VIDEO ▶ NO MORE FIRE DRILLS

Watch the author speak on shifting the time horizon to focus on the longer term.

that band to harmonize together requires being intentional about building trust and respect and adopting language and processes that weave people into a cohesive team.

A lot can get in the way of teams working together well. Organizational development and management expert Patrick Lencioni, in his book *The Five Dysfunctions of a Team,* does a fine job of spelling out problems common to teams and what to do to fix them. According to Lencioni, the most common issues that make teams dysfunctional include an absence of trust, the fear of conflict, a lack of commitment, the avoidance of accountability, and an inattentiveness to results.

Lencioni's medicine for these maladies is his pyramid of the five elements of cohesiveness, with Trust at the base and Results at the top:

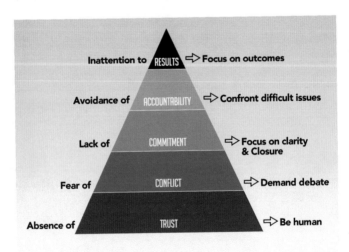

Trust. Team leaders are transparent and genuine with each other. That creates a safe environment in which trust can grow.

Conflict. If team members trust each other, they can engage in unfiltered, constructive debate about ideas without fearing that disagreements will lead to alienation.

Commitment. When team leaders feel heard and respected, they're more likely to commit to decisions wholeheartedly.

Accountability. Once team leaders are committed to a clear plan of action, they are more willing to hold one another accountable for what they've agreed to do.

Results. The ultimate goal of a cohesive leadership team is building on the other principles to achieve the agreed-upon results to which all are committed and held accountable for realizing.

At Mastering Midsized, we incorporate this philosophy in our consulting work to help companies improve their leadership teams.

For example, at HdL , the California company that provides revenue, audit, and operations services for local government agencies, the co-owners relied on the cohesiveness of its top leadership team to devise a succession plan at the same time as continuing to grow the business.

As part of a long-term exit strategy to prepare for retirement, HdL's two co-owners had implemented an employee stock ownership plan (ESOP) in December of 2007, creating a path for employees to buy out the co-owners' interest. To ensure that the value of those shares didn't vanish when the owners did, they needed a smooth transition. The co-owners created a new top-level leadership team to help direct it, one that included existing leaders as well as leaders they brought in from outside.

The co-owners delegated the tasks and responsibilities that come with owning a business to the new leaders, creating an ownership culture. The team, led by CEO Andy Nickerson (who had come up through the leadership ranks at HdL), worked collaboratively to pursue an aggressive growth strategy. Nickerson and other top leaders committed to a business plan and met monthly to review progress, which helped the group bond. Communication and teamwork increased, deepened by attending workshops on team cohesion and strategic planning.

The full implementation of the changes the succession plan called for took a full decade, during which the company continued to grow. By 2017, HdL had tripled its top line by selling new services and acquiring companies that, for the first time, expanded its territory beyond California. Since then,

HdL has acquired a software company, solidified new strategic partnerships, and added independent board members. By 2021, neither of the original founders have any ownership nor are in leadership roles.

"Taking 10 years to change our company into a team-led growth machine seems slow," Nickerson says. "On the other hand, each year at some level our culture and leadership changed. We took it one step at a time, even though we were eager to arrive where we are today. In the end, we preserved the best of what our founders created along with new energy and high expectations."

At Advice Media, the top leadership team works so well together that CEO Shawn Miele is happy to give them space to take a project and run with it. For example, when an outside vendor's application inside an Advice Media product suite fell behind the industry standard, threatening its market share, a team run by leaders from engineering, account management, and digital marketing functions drew up specs for an in-house version of the application

CASE STUDY ▶ HOW HDL MADE ITS ESOP WORK

HdL's succession planning increased communication, teamwork, and commitment to its business plan. Read about their strategic approach in detail.

in question, built it, and converted existing clients to the new software. The team saved the day for the company, "and I had absolutely zero involvement," Miele says.

How strategic delegation makes it all possible

In Chapter 2, I laid out how strategic delegation fits into professional development. It's also important in the development of teams—so much so that it's worth another look.

As I define it, strategic delegation is assigning tasks in a deliberate, intentional way to help people gain the knowledge or experience they will need to take over for someone higher up in the company.

When I talk about strategic delegation in the context of leadership teams, it covers leaders at all levels delegating work to their direct reports, and it includes delegating roles on teams. Direct reports must build trust with new teammates, including their manager's teammates if they are to truly become prepared to step up.

How do you make this work? Involve your teammates in the process of development by asking for their support of teaming with your direct report as you shift your focus elsewhere. In growing midsized companies, teams are everywhere, and they're dynamic, changing drivers of growth.

Leaders can use strategic delegation to carve out time to focus on the future by delegating responsibilities with shorter time horizons to their direct reports. You do this one task at a time to one top leader at a time. And that brings me to a final key point about the team leadership model.

Convert One Leadership Position at a Time

Most companies can't move from hub-and-spoke to team-leader model in one fell swoop. That puts too big a burden on an owner or CEO who may already feel overwhelmed handling the business's day-to-day operations and long-term strategy. Such a transition also may incur too heavy a financial burden—especially for companies on the smaller end of the midsized-company spectrum.

A more practical approach is for the CEO to pick one or two functions where replacing helpers with effective leaders would fuel the most growth. Then, move quickly to upgrade those positions. If you already have a person in that spot who's a high-potential employee, coaching can bring them up to the team-leader level. Otherwise, hire from outside.

The CEO must be clear about a new leader's focus and direction. Follow my suggestions for using a One Page Business Plan to get those new leaders up to speed on their duties and goals and articulate how their work aligns and advances with the business's strategic plans.

Employ strategic delegation, one-on-one coaching, and other professional development to help new leaders deliver successfully. Once one or two leaders are up to speed and driving growth, you can afford the time and energy to upgrade the next one or two. Continue to do that until you have a team that represents all functions or departments and they're working as a close-knit team toward common goals.

Enjoying the fruits of team leadership

As midsized companies grow, an owner or CEO should strive to surround themselves with top team leaders who know more about their particular area of expertise than the CEO. When you have those people in place, the CEO ceases to be the company's leading expert on everything. Instead, the CEO becomes the ringmaster, directing the show. If you founded the business, it is certainly not how you operated when you started, but it's how you need to develop as a leader to keep the company growing.

I vividly recall the first time I added a leader to my team. I was running my first company, Bentley Publishing Group. I hired someone to lead sales. After only a few months on the job, he walked into my office with an idea that ultimately led to hundreds of thousands of dollars in new business. I never would have thought of it. But he did, fusing his experience with his fresh understanding of our company's sales focus. It was like a flash of lightning, accelerating our growth and feeding our bottom line.

At that moment, and from that day forward, I became a believer in surrounding myself with other leaders. You, too, will see and feel the value as you give up the small-company hub-and-spoke paradigm and embrace team leadership.

MORE TEAM LEADERSHIP RESOURCES

We've studied the subject of team leadership in emerging midsized companies for some time. If you want to dive in more, scan the QR code for more articles and research, assessments, and other assistance.

MORE COPIES OF THIS BOOK?

Does someone you know need to read this chapter? Of course, you can order a book for them online, but if they're out of stock, or you need quantities, want to drop ship to many different locations, or this is related to a peer group or speaking event, scan this code.

WANT *TO TALK* ABOUT LEADING WITH A TEAM?

Mastering Midsized provides support and

 guidance for midsized companies who need to improve their teamwork. Scan this QR code for the fastest route to talk to someone about getting help.

AUDIO DOWNLOAD OF THIS CHAPTER

Listen to author Robert Sher read this chapter. Scan this QR code to instantly download and play on your device.

CONCLUSION

rowing from a small to a midsized company is not simply about increasing revenue. It's about implementing more sophisticated systems and strategies to help the company grow and sustain that growth. It's about strategizing and planning for longer time horizons to identify critical opportunities sooner. It's about transformation, and transformation cannot happen if a company doesn't change its people practices.

For a small business to become midsized, or for a midsized company to get bigger, CEOs must take a more considered and assertive approach to recruiting and developing people. And CEOs must delegate responsibilities to a top leadership team so the CEO has the time to focus on those longer, more complex horizons.

Here's another way to look at it, one that maps to the people drivers of growth that I've outlined in these pages. To become midsized or to continue to expand, a CEO must change:

	From	To
Recruiting	Hiring at the last minute or as a last resort	Recruiting and hiring consistently and deliberately
Developing Talent	Explaining tasks to subordinates	Developing high-potentials and other employees to take on the responsibilities needed for organizational growth
Leading with Teams	An individual leader directing "helpers"	Overseeing team-based leaders who work together to advance the organization's plans

Philosophy: To succeed, midsized companies must adopt leading practices in all three people drivers

Midsized companies aren't just startups or small companies that have gotten bigger. Neither are they miniature versions of large enterprises. They're a different breed of business altogether. Because their operations are more complex than those of a small business, midsized companies must take a more deliberate approach to hiring. They must bring on people who can and want to grow. That's the definition of a high-potential employee. Companies must provide the professional development that turns these high-potential employees into the leaders who can contribute to future growth. And to make the most of their investment in recruiting and professional development, owners or CEOs must learn to lead in a new way, forgoing the hub-and-spoke model common to startups and smaller companies in favor of delegating responsibilities to a top leadership team. Once CEOs put these people drivers in place, they are in an excellent position to adopt the other six drivers I outlined that are vital to grow, those that pertain to planning and execution, and go-to-market. The sooner you get the people part right, the sooner you can get to work implementing other growth drivers, and the better off the midsized business will be.

The essential people drivers

Let's take a final look at the three people drivers. If CEOs embraces the first two—recruiting and developing people strategically—the overall level of talent in the organization inevitably rises. And the first two drivers set up the third: the transformation of helpers into leaders.

Chapter 1. Recruiting—It's the Talent, Stupid

Just as a sprinkling of fertilizer coaxes flowers to bloom faster and more lushly, recruiting gives companies the edge they need to outgrow the competition. That's why savvy CEOs direct as many resources as they can into improving their recruiting efforts. Midsized companies that I've worked with that grew successfully upped their recruiting game by adopting three practices:

■ They use the same sales and marketing techniques to acquire customers as they do to attract new employees. For example, they create personas to describe their ideal job candidates and use those descriptions to write on-target job ads. They understand what makes their business different and can articulate it in a way that appeals to job seekers who would like to be part of such an environment. They have some type of recruiting outreach going at all times to keep the funnel of potential job candidates well stocked.

■ They have a recruiting short game for when they need to find people in a hurry. The heart of their short game is putting someone in charge of hiring—preferably a dedicated in-house recruiter who knows the ropes or can quickly get up to speed. That person writes on-point job ads and runs the interview process, working hand in hand with hiring managers and top leaders who make hiring decisions. The process is coordinated, with everyone who interviews job candidates using the same questions and criteria. And they strive to create a positive experience so the candidate is excited about the company and the job. All this works to reduce time-to-hire.

■ They keep the long game in mind. Midsized companies that are effective recruiters depend on long-term strategies that yield a perpetual list of candidates who'd jump at the chance to join the business. Long-term strategies start with an authentic employer brand that the company lives by and lets the world know about to attract like-minded prospects. Another building block of the long game is a recruiting budget that's written, reviewed yearly, and includes spending on outside recruiters as needed. Midsized companies that are great recruiters keep in touch with promising prospects so these people think of the business first when they're job hunting. Finally, once these companies figure out strategies that work, they resist the urge to tinker with them too much.

Chapter 2. A Commonsense Guide to Professional Development

Midsized companies on a fast-track to growth have figured out that high-potential employees are the premium fuel that will get them there. For that reason, they devote a great deal of time and money to professional development to cultivate those employees. High-potentials are people who're ready, willing, and able to take on more duties. They're eager to do what it takes to move up in the organization. The midsized companies that excel at developing high-potential employees employ a variety of tactics:

- They create career paths that lay out the new responsibilities and positions that employees can aspire to and the skills they will need to get there. They design career paths both for leadership positions and for employees who'd rather become technical experts. And they connect those career paths to the company's planned trajectory, so that when people gain new skills it benefits both individuals and the business as a whole.

■ These companies believe in strategic delegation, assigning people to tasks they must master to rise in the organization. And they practice it at all levels of the organization so people are constantly learning and continually moving up.

■ They take mentoring seriously, creating formal programs through which people can share their accumulated institutional knowledge among senior-level and junior-level people or between peers, offices, teams, functions, and departments.

■ Smart midsized companies don't limit high-potential employees' professional development to what they can learn inside the business. When the need arises, they provide people with external training. They pay for people to join peer-to-peer support groups, enroll them in programs for emerging leaders, and provide individual coaching.

As I mentioned in the introduction, a key growth driver for midsized companies is being data driven.

This applies to companies' people practices as well as to their operations. Midsized companies that have excelled in professional development practices track people's progress and stand ready to help them shore up their weak points. This tracking comes in the form of well-thought-out rubrics and reviews to evaluate employee performance and is used in a way that's beneficial to both the business and the individual.

Chapter 3. The Journey from "I" to "We" Leadership

Owners of small businesses say "Jump" and employees say "How high?" Isn't that what any founder or CEO thinks he wants? Well, as companies grow, and their operations and challenges become more multiform and complex, that leadership style just doesn't cut it. It won't work. It can't. It doesn't. To thrive, owners or CEOs of midsized companies really have no choice but to adopt a team-leadership model, where they collaborate with a cohesive group of top department leaders and delegate responsibilities to them. That frees up the CEO to think about the future (and powerfully motivates the other, empowered leaders), which is vital for an organization's long-term growth.

As I've worked with scores of midsized companies I've learned that just about any organization can overcome just about any obstacle to moving to a team-based leadership model if they use the following as a foundation:

- A written business plan and review process. One page is plenty, as long as it outlines the company's vision, strategies, and actions needed to reach the goals, along with a schedule for regularly reviewing and updating the plan.

- Team leaders who can get the job done. Leaders at all levels have to be fit for duty or open to coaching and/or mentoring.

- A top leader who focuses on the future. To shift her focus to longer time horizons, the owner or CEO has to block out the time for it, delegating responsibility for short-term work to top leaders.

- A top leadership team that works well together. The basis for great teamwork is trust. With trust, teams can establish a bond that allows them to work through difficulties toward common goals.

- Strategic delegation. This concept of moving responsibilities and tasks down a level to prepare people for their next position is so important that I keep coming back to it.

It's common to think of a leader as the master and commander of the fleet. Some leaders imagine themselves standing on the ship's bridge as the waves crash and the winds blow, shouting out orders to the rank and file. But I wrote this book for CEOs who live in the real world, not fantasyland. Those people understand the importance of developing collaborative relationships with their teams and understand that that's what drives growth and success. By cultivating a collaborative culture, they become servant leaders, alert to the needs of both their people and their organizations. By adopting a servant leader mentality, a CEO can help people learn, which is essential for business growth. Learning is the ultimate people driver.

Getting started

I developed my general theory of key midsized company growth drivers, and the three people drivers laid out in this book, over the course of working with hundreds of midsized companies. Theories they may be—I haven't done academic research and studies— but, more importantly, I've seen them work.

By now, you may be so pumped up by the concepts I've outlined and the steps to implement them that you're itching to start acting on all of them all at once. I don't recommend it. For starters, it could feel a bit overwhelming to your crew. Starts are predictably messy, and most of the steps and tactics I've outlined are entwined with others. Changing one, you change many other things. So, getting started usually entails some compromise between adopting best practices and understanding what you can realistically achieve given your particular and unique circumstances.

Here's what I do recommend:

Start where you are. I know from client work there's no such thing as a clean slate. Companies (not including startups) usually have long-time employees set in their ways and resistant to most changes. You may have financial constraints or other barriers that limit what you can accomplish. The Big Bang may be how our universe began; it's not how you should.

My advice is to take all that into account and start realistically, working toward your goals from there. When JLG Architects first embraced people drivers, the firm started small. Out of necessity. The four equity partners had to run the firm's day-to-day business while also taking steps to expand. They began by increasing their recruiting efforts at a local university with which the firm had a relationship. They created an employee peer group that, among other things, helped new hires get their architectural licenses faster. This buoyed the company's growth without adding significant expense.

Sometimes good enough is good enough. Don't shoot for perfect. Instead, set realistic expectations and work from there.

In our client work, we've helped CEOs deal with employees with entrenched habits. That was the case at the wholesale foods distributor whose owner was so frustrated with the lack of growth at the business he was ready to sell. We introduced him and his team to One Page Business Plans®, which they used to kick off a major turnaround. We've helped companies with financial limitations adopt other people drivers. And we've helped CEOs steer their companies to achieve long-term goals that aren't always about boosting revenue or profits. For HdL, it was to carry out a decade-long succession plan that shifted ownership from co-founders, who were nearly retirement age, to an ESOP led by a new generation of leaders.

Strive for continuous improvement. You may start with good enough, but don't stop there. As rapidly as you can, keep making changes to these three drivers.

Ultimately, it's people who drive the other growth drivers—not plans, technology, more equipment, new customers or processes in isolation. But if you don't have the *right* people to plan, operate the technology, run the equipment, sell, and learn the new processes, your company won't grow.

FREE ASSESSMENTS

We have created a quick free assessment on each chapter. These are many of the questions we'd ask as consultants to understand where a client company stands on its use of these leading practices.

Too many midsized company CEOs are starved for the talent that they need to expand. But you don't have to go hungry. The recipe for success is within reach—if you use the ingredients that I've set out here, and the instructions for how to stir them into the pot.

And then you and the people you work with can enjoy the feast.

APPENDIX

··

(Research Background)

Research Participants

The leaders of the following companies participated in our research:

Company Name	Name	Title	Industry
ADCO Companies, LTD	Grant Carter	VP Operations and Finance	Industrial Sales and Service
Advice Media	Shawn Miele	CEO	Digital Marketing
AGM Container Controls	Tom Christie	CFO	Defense & Space
Air Techniques International (ATI)	Ron Adkins	President	Electrical & Electronic Manufacturing
Albeck Gerken	Jeff Gerken	President	Transportation Engineering
Alliance of Chief Executives	Paul Witkay	Founder & CEO	CEO Organization
American Highway, A Simplex Compa	Rnoyn Meskis	CEO	Manufacturing
Arborwell	Peter Sortwell	Founder & CEO	Facilities Services
ART19	Patrick Milholland	CIO	Media
Ascent Environmental	Gary Jakobs	President/CEO	Environmental Services
Berkeley Cement	Ron Fadelli	President	Construction
Boiler Supply	Eddie Lunn	President	Industrial Equipment Sales and Service
BSC Group	Sean O'Brien	President & CEO	Multidisciplinary Consulting
BVOH Search & Consulting	Leslie Boudreaux	Sr. Managing Partner	Staffing and Recruiting
ConnectAndSell, Inc.	Chris Beall	CEO	Computer Software
Corefact	Chris Burnley	CEO	Marketing & Advertising
DevCo	Jack Hunden	President	Commercial Real Estate
Educational Data Systems, Inc. (EDSI)	Kevin Schnieders	Chief Servant Leader/CEO	Professional Training & Coaching

Company Name	Name	Title	Industry
Equipment Controls Company (ECCO)	Tod Bradley	COO	Wholesale
E-Therapy	Harris Larney	CEO	Online Therapy
Extron Inc.	Sandeep Duggal	CEO	Logistics & Supply Chain
Fiducient Advisors B	ob DiMeo	CEO	Financial Services
Fireclay Tile	Eric Edelson	CEO	Design
Folio3	Adnan Lawai	Founder and CEO	Computer Software
Frigorifico y Almacen del Turabo, Inc. (Oscar Super Cash & Carry)	Carlos Toro	President	Wholesale Grocery
Future State	Kathy Krumpe	COO	Management Consulting
Giffels Webster	Scott Clein	President/Partner	Civil Engineering/Surveying/Landscape Architecture
Giroux Glass	Nataline Lomedico	CEO and President	Construction
Haaker Equipment Co.	Robin Haaker	President	Equipment Dealer
HdL Companies	Andy Nickerson	CEO	Government Administration
Helmet House	Dave Betram	CEO S	porting Goods
Hoge Fenton Jones & Appel	Sblend Sblendorio	Attorney	Law Practice
Howard/Stein-Hudson Associates	Robert Dankese	CFO	Traffic & Civil Engineering Services
Ideal Innovations	Richard Syretz	COO	Defense & Space
JLG Architects	Michelle Mongeon Allen	CEO	Architecture & Planning
Kevin Barry Art Advisory	Allison Barry	President	Design

Company Name	Name	Title	Industry
Koshland Pharm	Peter Koshland	CEO	Pharmaceuticals
Landau Associates	Chip Halbert	CEO	Environmental Services
Larson Design Group	Adanma Akujieze	CFO and Treasurer	Engineering & Architecture
Levelset	Scott Wolfe	CEO	Computer Software
Lexington Manufacturing	Mike Dillon	President	Paper and Forest Products
Life-Assist, Inc.	Ramona Davis	President/CEO	Medical Supply Distribution
MBH Architects	Dennis Heath	Founding Principal	Architecture & Planning
Miles Technologies	JP Lessard	President, Software Services	Information Technology & Services
Mob Scene	Brett Abbey	CFO	Entertainment
Mountz, Inc.	Brad Mountz	CEO	Manufacturing
National Discount Textiles Inc. (Barebones WorkWear)	Stu Nelson	CEO	Apparel & Fashion
North Ridge Development	Pat Mah	Operations Manager	Construction
OBMI	Mike Wilson	President/COO	Architecture & Planning
P2S (MEP Eng.)	Kevin Peterson	President & CEO	Construction
Pacific OneSource Inc dba STS Education	Marc Netka	CEO	Education Technology & Services
Paragon Laboratories, Inc.	John Parmentier	President & Owner	Testing Laboratory
Pennoni	Joe Viscuso Sr.	VP, Director of Strategic Growth	Consulting Engineers
Pinchin Ltd.	Jeff Grossi	CEO	Environmental Services

Company Name	Name	Title	Industry
Proforma Corporation	Jeff Antrim	President	Construction
ProServeIT Corp	Eric Sugar	President	Information Technology & Services
Real-Time Innovations	Stan Schneider	CEO	Computer Software
Rimon P.C.	Jim Chapman	Partner	Law Practice
Ryan Gootee General Contractors	Michael DeGruy	COO	Construction
School Apparel, Inc.	Dave Weil	CEO	Apparel Manufacturing and Distributing
Scott+Cormia Architects and Interiors LLC	Ray Scott	Principal	Architecture & Planning
Solomon Group	Gary Solomon, Jr.	President	Event & Exhibit Production
Spraggins Incorporated	Michael L. Spraggins	CEO	Building Products
SSM Industries	Scott Hilleary	President & CEO	Construction
Strategic Factory	Keith Miller	CEO	Marketing & Advertising
SurvTech Solutions	David O'Brien	President	Geospatial
Tactical Air Support	RC Thompson	CEO	Aviation & Aerospace
Tangent Logic	Gil Henzel	CEO	Software Development Consulting
Towne Group LLC	Colin McKillop	CEO	Management Consulting
Trihydro Corporation	Kurt Tuggle	President/CEO	Environmental Services
UsedCardboardBoxes & UCBZeroWaste (UCB)	Marty Metro	Founder/CEO	Packaging & Containers
VCA Consultants	Tom VanDorpe	President/CEO Professional	Services/Engineering

Company Name	Name	Title	Industry
VHB	Michael McArdle	Chief Development Officer	Consulting Engineers
Warren & Baerg Mfg., Inc.	Randy Baerg	President	Manufacturing
York Wallcoverings	Brian Golden	CEO	Wallcoverings

NOTES

· ·

Introduction

1   National Center for the Middle Market, "About Us", accessed April 23, 2021, https://www. middlemarketcenter .org/about

2   Doug Farren and Anil K. Makhija, "The Middle Market is Stressed, But Resilient," *Harvard Business Review* (March 8, 2021), accessed April 22, 2021, https://hbr.org/2021/03/the-middle-market-is-stressed-but-resilient

3   Farren and Makhija, *The Middle Market is Stressed, But Resilient.*

4   Farren and Makhija, *The Middle Market is Stressed, But Resilient.*

5   Robert Sher, *Mighty Midsized Companies: How Leaders overcome 7 Silent Growth Killers* (Routledge, 2016).

6   National Center for the Middle Market, *The DNA of Middle Market Growth*, accessed April 23, 2021, http:// www. middlemarketcenter.org/Media/Documents/ three-types-of-growth-champions-and-factors-that-drive-success_three-types-of-growth-champions-and-factors-that-drive-success_NCMM_DNA_of_Growth_ Web.pdf

Chapter 1

1   National Center for the Middle Market, *Building the Top Team: How Middle Market Firms Attract and Retain the Top Talent that Fuels their Success,* accessed April 22, 2021, https://www.middlemarketcenter. org/Media/Documents/how-middle-market-firms-attract-and-retain-the-top-talent-that-fuels-their-success_NCMM_Talent_Research_Report _WEB.pdf

2   Martha Ross and Marek Gootman, "Help Wanted: How Middle Market Companies Can Address Workforce Challenges to Find and Develop the Talent they Need to Grow," *Brookings* (August 29, 2017), accessed April 22, 2021, https://www.brookings.edu/research/ brookings-ncmm-report/

3   NCMM, *Building the Top Team: How Middle Market Firms Attract and Retain the Top Talent that Fuels their Success,* 7.

4   NCMM, *Building the Top Team: How Middle Market Firms Attract and Retain the Top Talent that Fuels their Success,* 6-7.

5   Bradford D. Smart, *Topgrading,* 3rd ed. (New York, NY: Portfolio, 2012).

6   NCMM, *Building the Top Team: How Middle Market Firms Attract and Retain the Top Talent that Fuels their Success,* 10.

7   NCMM, *Building the Top Team: How Middle Market Firms Attract and Retain the Top Talent that Fuels their Success,* 16.

8   HNN Communities, "HNN Employee Testimonial: Chris Guinn," accessed February 15, 2021, https://www .lifeisbetterhere.com/ careers.aspx

9   Robert Sher, "Building Employer Brand", CEO to CEO Inc., accessed March 1, 2021, https://www. ceotoceo .biz/your-personal-portal/video-building-an-employer-brand-to-attract-the-best-candidates/

Chapter 2

1   Ross and Gootman, *Help Wanted: How Middle Market Companies Can Address Workforce Challenges to Find and Develop the Talent they Need to Grow,* 11

2   Ross and Gootman, *Help Wanted: How Middle Market Companies Can Address Workforce Challenges to Find and Develop the Talent they Need to Grow,* 11

Chapter 3

1   Vineet Nayar, "Don't Let Outdated Management Structures Kill Your Company," *Harvard Business Review* (February 10, 2016), accessed April 11, 2021, https://hbr.org/2016/02/dont-let-outdated-management-structures-kill-your-company#

2   Patrick Lencioni, The Five Dysfunctions of a Team (Hoboken, NJ: Jossey-Bass, 2002).

REFERENCES

Allen, Michelle. Interview by author. Zoom. July 5, 2019.

Ballas, Sam. Interview by author. Zoom. May 10, 2019.

Barry, Allison. Interview by author. Zoom. January 27, 2021.

Betram, Dave. Interview by author. Zoom. June 3, 2019.

Bowen, Susan. Interview by author. Zoom. November 23, 2020.

Clein, Scott. Interview by author. Zoom. March 10, 2020.

Doug Farren and Anil K. Makhija, "The Middle Market is Stressed, But Resilient." *Harvard Business Review*, March 8, 2021, accessed April 22, 2021. https://hbr.org/2021/03/the-middle-market-is-stressed-but-resilie nt

Edelson, Eric. Interview by author. Zoom. May 19, 2019.

Heath, Dennis. Interview by author. Zoom. February 24, 2020.

HNN Communities. "HNN Employee Testimonial: Chris Guinn." Accessed February 15, 2021. https://www .lifeisbetterhere.com/ careers.aspx

Jakobs, Gary. Interview by author. Zoom. August 1, 2019.

Krumpe, Kathy. Interview by author. Zoom. April 19, 2019.

Lawai, Adnan. Interview by author. Zoom. April 15, 2019.

Lencioni, Patrick. *The Five Dysfunctions of a Team*. Hoboken, NJ: Jossey-Bass, 2002.

Lomedico, Nataline. Interview by author. Zoom. April 29, 2019.

Mah, Pat. Interview by author. Zoom. April 8, 2019.

McKillop, Colin. Interview by author. Zoom. December 2, 2019.

Miele, Shawn. Interview by author. Zoom. June 3, 2020.

Montgomery, Nick. Interview by author. Zoom. November 3, 2019.

National Center for the Middle Market, "About Us". https:// www.middlemarketcenter.org/about

National Center for the Middle Market. *Building the Top Team: How Middle Market Firms Attract and Retain the*

Top Talent that Fuels their Success, accessed April 22, 2021. https://www. middlemarketcenter.org/Media/Documents/ how-middle-market-firms-attract-and-retain-the-top-talent-that-fuels-their-success_ NCMM_Talent_Research_ Report_W EB.pdf

National Center for the Middle Market. *The DNA of Middle Market Growth.* http://www.middlemarketcenter.org/ Media/Documents/thre e-types-of-growth-champions-and-factors-that-drive-success_three-types-of-growth-champions-and-factors-that-drive-success_NCMM _DNA_of_ Growth_Web.pdf

Nayar, Vineet. "Don't Let Outdated Management Structures Kill Your Company," *Harvard Business Review*, February 10, 2016, accessed April 21, 2021. https://hbr.org/2016/02/ dont-let-outdated-management-structur es-kill-your-company#

Ortiz, Fred. Interview by author. Zoom. July 16, 2019.

Peterson, Kevin. Interview by author. Zoom. April 29, 2019.

Robert Sher. "Building Employee Brand", *CEO to CEO Inc.*, accessed March 1, 2021. https://www.ceotoceo.biz/your-personal-portal/ video-building-an-employer-brand-to-attract-the-best-candidates/

Robert Sher. *Mighty Midsized Companies: How Leaders overcome 7 Silent Growth Killers.* Routledge, 2016.

Ross, Martha and Gootman, Marek. "Help Wanted: How Middle Market Companies Can Address Workforce Challenges to Find and Develop the Talent they Need to Grow," *Brookings*, August 29, 2017, accessed April 22, 2021. https://www.brookings.edu/research/brookings-ncmm-report/

Sblendo, Sblend. Interview by author. Zoom. February 7, 2020.

Schnieders, Kevin. Interview by author. Zoom. April 17, 2019.

Senescall, Shawn. Interview by author. Zoom. May 9, 2019.

Sortwell, Peter. Interview by author. Zoom. February 19, 2019.

Stevens, Matt. Interview by author. Zoom. May 20, 2019.

Sugar, Eric. Interview by author. Zoom. April 8, 2019.

Syretz, Richard. Interview by author. Zoom. June 4, 2019.

Taylor, Kimberly. Interview by author. Zoom. March 5, 2020.

Tuggle, Kurt and Bauder, Emily. Interview by author. Zoom. January 25, 2021.

INDEX

. . . .

Italized Text: name of person, company, website, etc.

t: table

f: figure, illustration

ABOUT THE AUTHOR

A s an operating CEO and consultant, I'm obsessed with answering the question: What drives growth for midsized companies?

I founded my consulting firm Mastering Midsized to provide leaders of midsized businesses with advice on how to maximize growth—and do it in a way that is sustainable and predictable.

My quest began after I built and sold a midsized art publishing business, Bentley Publishing Group. I discovered a gap in the market: there were management consultants at major firms focused on big businesses and countless coaches and consultants focused on the small business market, but I found almost no one offering hands-on operating experience and relevant expertise to midsized firms. I knew I could make an impact.

I began to codify what made the biggest difference in driving midsized growth. Through years of client engagements and hundreds of interviews for my books and articles, I noticed a pattern. There are three areas of focus and nine drivers of growth that make the biggest difference. This book covers the first three, and I'm working on the next two books in this series.

I enjoy writing and sharing my knowledge. I publish regularly in Forbes and have published numerous articles in Harvard Business Review. I've also written three books that crystalize what I've learned about running, growing and profitably exiting midsized firms:

- This one: Driving Midsized Growth: People

- Mighty Midsized Companies

- The Feel of the Deal

The insight into what it takes to create real mastery in midsized firms—how to lead, how to plan, and how to implement—now infuses everything we do as a firm.

I'm a San Francisco Bay Area native and an alumni of Hayward State University. I got my MBA from St. Mary's, where I also taught MBA courses.

My wife Renee and I have two grown children, Ben and Jessie, and we still live in the Bay Area. We love sailing, hiking and travel.